British Trade Unions, 1800–1875

Prepared for
The Economic History Society by

A. E. MUSSON

Senior Lecturer in Economic History
in the University of Manchester

MACMILLAN

First published 1972 by
THE MACMILLAN PRESS LTD
London and Basingstoke
Associated companies in New York Toronto
Dublin Melbourne Johannesburg and Madras

SBN 333 13701 9

Printed in Great Britain by
THE ANCHOR PRESS LTD
Tiptree, Essex

ST ES ECONOMIC H

This series, specially commissioned by the Economic History Society, focuses attention on the main problems of economic history. Recently there has been a great deal of detailed research and reinterpretation, some of it controversial, but it has remained largely inaccessible to students or buried in academic journals. This series is an attempt to provide a guide to the current interpretations of the key themes of economic history in which advances have recently been made, or in which there has been significant debate.

Each book will survey recent work, indicate the full scope of the particular problem as it has been opened by research and distinguish what conclusions can be drawn in the present state of knowledge. Both old and recent work will be reviewed critically, but each book will provide a balanced survey rather than an exposition of the author's own viewpoint.

The series as a whole will give readers access to the best work done, help them to draw their own conclusions in some major fields and, by means of the critical bibliography in each book, guide them in the selection of further reading. The aim is to provide a springboard to further work and not a set of pre-packaged conclusions or short cuts.

STUDIES IN ECONOMIC HISTORY

Edited for the Economic History Society by
M. W. Flinn

PUBLISHED

B. W. E. Alford Depression and Recovery? British Economic Growth, 1918–1939
M. W. Flinn British Population Growth, 1700–1850
R. H. Hilton The Decline of Serfdom in Medieval England
E. L. Jones The Development of English Agriculture, 1815–1873
J. D. Marshall The Old Poor Law, 1795–1834
Alan S. Milward The Economic Effects of the Two World Wars on Britain
G. E. Mingay Enclosure and the Small Farmer in the Age of the Industrial Revolution
A. E. Musson British Trade Unions, 1800–1875
R. B. Outhwaite Inflation in Tudor and Early Stuart England
Michael E. Rose The Relief of Poverty, 1834–1914
S. B. Saul The Myth of the Great Depression, 1873–1896

TITLES IN PREPARATION INCLUDE

S. D. Chapman The Cotton Industry in the Industrial Revolution
P. Cottrell British Overseas Investment in the Nineteenth Century
R. Davis English Overseas Trade, 1500–1700
M. E. Falkus The Industrialisation of Russia, 1700–1914
J. R. Hay The Origins of the Liberal Welfare Reforms, 1905–1914
R. M. Mitchison British Population Growth, 1850–1950
P. L. Payne British Entrepreneurship in the Nineteenth Century
S. B. Saul The Econometric Approach to Economic History
A. J. Taylor Laissez-faire and State Intervention in Nineteenth-Century Britain

Contents

Editor's Preface

SO long as the study of economic history was confined to only a small group at a few universities, its literature was not prolific and its few specialists had no great problem in keeping abreast of the work of their colleagues. Even in the 1930s there were only two journals devoted exclusively to this field. But the high quality of the work of the economic historians during the inter-war period and the post-war growth in the study of the social sciences sparked off an immense expansion in the study of economic history after the Second World War. There was a great expansion of research and many new journals were launched, some specialising in branches of the subject like transport, business or agricultural history. Most significantly, economic history began to be studied as an aspect of history in its own right in schools. As a consequence, the examining boards began to offer papers in economic history at all levels, while textbooks specifically designed for the school market began to be published.

For those engaged in research and writing this period of rapid expansion of economic history studies has been an exciting, if rather breathless one. For the larger numbers, however, labouring in the outfield of the schools and colleges of further education, the excitement of the explosion of research has been tempered by frustration caused by its vast quantity and, frequently, its controversial character. Nor, it must be admitted, has the ability or willingness of the academic economic historians to generalise and summarise marched in step with their enthusiasm for research.

The greatest problems of interpretation and generalisation have tended to gather round a handful of principal themes in economic history. It is, indeed, a tribute to the sound sense of economic historians that they have continued to dedicate their energies, however inconclusively, to the solution of these key problems. The results of this activity, however, much of it stored away in a wide range of academic journals, have tended to remain inaccessible to many of those currently interested in the subject. Recognising the need for guidance through the burgeoning and confusing literature that has grown around these basic topics, the Economic History Society decided to launch this series of small books. The books are intended to serve as guides to current interpretations in important fields of economic history in which important advances have recently been made, or in which there has recently been some significant debate. Each book aims to survey recent work, to indicate the full scope of the particular problem as it has been opened up by recent scholarship, and to draw such conclusions as seem warranted, given the present state of knowledge and understanding. The authors will often be at pains to point out where, in their view, because of a lack of information or inadequate research, they believe it is premature to attempt to draw firm conclusions. While authors will not hesitate to review recent and older work critically, the books are not intended to serve as vehicles for their own specialist views: the aim is to provide a balanced summary rather than an exposition of the author's own viewpoint. Each book will include a descriptive bibliography.

In this way the series aims to give all those interested in economic history at a serious level access to recent scholarship in some major fields. Above all, the aim is to help the reader to draw his own conclusions, and to guide him in the selection of further reading as a means to this end, rather than to present him with a set of pre-packaged conclusions.

University of Edinburgh M. W. FLINN
Editor

REFERENCES in the text within square brackets refer to the numbered items in the Bibliography, followed, where necessary, by the page number, e.g. ([16] 264).

1 *Introduction*

IT is remarkable, indeed perhaps unique in historical studies, that a work which was originally published in 1894 (though later extended to 1920) still remains the standard textbook in its field. That the Webbs' great *History of Trade Unionism* still holds its place is a tribute to the immense research and interpretative insight on which it was based, but also perhaps an indication of the relative inferiority of later labour-historical scholarship. Twenty years ago, John Saville was deploring the decline in working-class history since the days of the Webbs, Cole and Beer in the early decades of this century [14]; he viewed the publication of Cole and Filson's *British Working-Class Movements: Select Documents, 1789–1875* (1951) as a belated but glorious sunset to this great era. Today, the Webbs' *History* still stands as a monumental piece of historical scholarship. There has meanwhile been a great deal of specialised research on particular aspects or periods – on many points the Webbs' evidence and interpretations have been revealed as inadequate – but no one has yet emerged with comparable breadth as well as depth of scholarship to rewrite the whole history of trade unionism over the past two centuries on the same academic level.

It seems very improbable, in fact, that anyone will, or that such a history could be adequately comprised within a single volume. Pelling's is the best recent general account, including much useful revision, but is on a comparatively modest scale [33]. Any labour historian, however, reviewing the present position of working-class history, would hardly take so gloomy a view of recent scholarship as did Saville in 1952. One has only to mention the names of Briggs, Clegg, Harrison (J. F. C. and R.), Hobsbawm, Pelling, Pollard and Thompson (in an alphabetical list which is by no means exhaustive), not forgetting Saville himself, to indicate what a wealth of talent has been applied in this field since the early 1950s, and in recent years many younger scholars have been jostling for position. Hobsbawm, therefore, reviewing trade-union historiography a dozen years after Saville, was more optimistic [28] : whilst agreeing that for the half-century after the Webbs' *History* progress had been 'disappointing', he remarked on the recent 'striking expansion of labour studies', its growing 'professional competence' and broader grasp of economic and social factors. There is now a mounting pile of books and articles; though gaps in our knowledge remain, many have been filled. But the general shape of the edifice produced by all these piecemeal alterations and additions is by no means clear. It is therefore the purpose of this booklet to review the evidence and interpretation relating to the seventy-five years between the passing of the Combination Acts of 1799 and 1800 and the legislation of the early 1870s, a period during which the foundations of the modern trade-union movement were firmly laid, but on which the Webbs' *History* is in most urgent need of revision.

The bulk of modern research into this period has been concerned with the social and political aspects of working-class history : the standard of living, social structure, class consciousness, Radicalism, Chartism, and the political reform movement of the 1860s. There has been much less research into trade-union developments; in fact the modern tendency has been to combine these with socio-political labour history. Left-wing historians particularly have been endeavouring to demonstrate the 'revolutionary potential' of broader working-class movements in the late eighteenth and early nineteenth centuries. They have lauded 'primitive rebels', violence, machine-breaking and mass demonstrations, and, like the Webbs, they have highlighted the attempts at 'general union' in the early 1830s, whilst being extremely critical of the 'pompous trades and proud mechanics' who held aloof in their sectional societies, more concerned with narrow 'trade' affairs and friendly benefits – the 'labour aristocrats' who, in their so-called 'New Model' unions, retreated from the prospects of political and social revolution.

No doubt there is much ideological interest and excitement in the broader aspects of working-class history. But over-emphasis on these has tended to obscure the very evident reality of separate, more limited, trade-union interests and organisation. These humdrum matters, relating to wages, hours, apprenticeship, etc., adjustments to technical change, gradual expansion of membership, and development of union structure, are less dramatic than 'revolutionary' movements or machine-breaking, but they are of more fundamental importance. Sectional trade societies were the most deeply-rooted, solid and continuous forms of working-class organisation in this period, and the basis of the later labour movement.

2 *Characteristics of Early Trade Unionism*

THE origins of trade unionism in the period 1800–75 are to be sought much deeper in history. The Webbs were well aware of this, tracing the growth of numerous local societies in handicraft trades before the Industrial Revolution. Modern critics of the Webbs, however, consider that 'they inadequately accounted for the emergence of trade unionism' in the eighteenth century, that they ignored the basic economic and social forces which created them, and that, being preoccupied with trade unions as 'continuous formal organisations', they neglected 'ephemeral action' [19]. Such criticism is not entirely fair, because the Webbs did appreciate the basic forces underlying the growth of trade unionism: they referred to the widening gulf between capital and labour, conflicting class interests, capitalist competition and exploitation, working-class grievances in regard to wages, apprenticeship, etc., and the breakdown of protective regulations, both of guild and state. They also emphasised that these conditions developed, and that trade societies consequently emerged, in traditional handicraft trades, in small workshops, before the growth of 'dark Satanic mills'. Workers were exploited under the domestic system long before the development of the factory system; there was not (as Engels, for example, imagined) an idyllic 'golden age' of handicraft before factory chimneys began to darken workers' lives.

No doubt, as Pollard has emphasised, the factory system did tend towards more intensive exploitation, with more regular (and perhaps longer) working hours, stricter discipline and more child labour. But as Clapham long ago emphasised, and as modern labour historians such as Thompson recognise ([16] chap. 6), factory workers were a small minority in the eighteenth and much of the nineteenth century: there were more cobblers, for example, than cotton spinners. It was among such handicraft workers that the earliest trade societies emerged, sometimes from a crumbling guild organisation, as did the journeymen printers from within the Stationers' Company [62, 63, 65], and these 'craft' societies of skilled tradesmen, with their apprenticeship regulations, entry fees and other 'labour aristocratic' features, with their sectional interests, formal organisation and methods of collective bargaining, long remained typical of trade unionism; indeed, they provided its basis until the late nineteenth century. The Webbs, therefore, were quite right to emphasise their importance, because they were, in fact, the first examples of continuous, successful working-class organisation and because for well over a century they included the bulk of trade-union membership and provided the pattern for trade-union development.

Nevertheless, there is some truth in Allen's criticisms of the Webbs' *History*. Their investigations into eighteenth-century origins were not very intensive, and their main concern was with developments from the passing of the Combination Acts of 1799 and 1800. But, as Allen pointed out, criticism is more justly directed 'at those who followed the Webbs', for only scrappy, piecemeal research has yet been done into the earlier period. Hobsbawm, despite his satisfaction with the striking recovery in trade-union historiography, points out, nevertheless, that 'eighteenth-century unionism or its equivalent has been hardly touched upon by labour historians since the Webbs surveyed it, except . . . by students of the printing trade whose documented history goes back so far' ([28] 32). There is still comparatively little to read on these early 'combinations' or 'trade clubs'. The most interesting evidence has been produced by Aspinall from the Home Office papers between 1790 and 1825, showing how numerous they were in trades all over the country, how they were organised, what their aims were, and how employers, local magistrates and Government dealt with them [1]. More recent researches have directed attention to the 'ephemeral' phenomena neglected by the Webbs and once considered outside the sphere of trade unionism. Hobsbawm's re-assessment of the role of machine-breakers' and the activities of 'primitive rebels' has demonstrated that riots, destruction of property and personal violence were not entirely senseless reactions to food shortages, rising prices, mechanisation or unemployment, but were often associated with emergent trade unionism, a kind of 'collective bargaining by riot', especially in trades where formal and continuous organisation had not yet developed, or where employers refused recognition, in a period when violence and 'mob' action were endemic ([12] chap. 2). Thus Luddism was not merely blind opposition to technical progress, 'outside the main currents of the development of Trade Unionism', as Cole and Filson still considered it not so very long ago ([2] 111), but appears to have been deliberate and, to some extent, justifiable policy by framework-knitters, croppers and other trade societies, in an effort to keep up wages and employment in a period of war-time dislocation, trade depression and high food prices [35]. (But cf. Thompson, who emphasises the political-revolutionary, class-warfare aspects of Luddism [16] 569–659.) Moreover, violence of this kind – not only against machinery, but also against employers' persons as well as property, and against non-unionist 'knobsticks', 'rats' or 'blacklegs' (in the form of beating-up, destroying work, stealing tools, vitriol throwing, attacks on houses, and even murders) – remained common far into the nineteenth century, in the power-loom riots of 1825, for example, in the cotton spinners' and miners' strikes of the late 1820s and early 1830s, and, more famously, in the 'outrages' in Sheffield and Manchester in the 1860s, although it was tending to die out from the 1840s onwards.

The Webbs' emphasis on formal trade-union organisation and development of collective bargaining certainly led them to neglect these more 'primitive' aspects, but during the nineteenth century such activities were increasingly confined to the more old-fashioned trade clubs, especially in declining trades, where trade unionism was weak and men were sometimes desperate. Present-day tendencies to discern heroic elements in such violent 'direct action', with its sometimes 'revolutionary' aspects, should not lead us to overlook the lawless destruction and brutalities involved, or to imagine that these were the characteristic methods of trade unionism, especially in the nineteenth century. The development of peaceful, constitutional collective bargaining, in place of such crude violence, was part of the progress from primitive barbarism to a more civilised society. Increasingly, as trade unions grew stronger, they condemned such acts.

The normal trade-society methods were to approach their employers verbally or in written 'memorials', and usually 'respectfully', to negotiate peacefully whenever possible, and, if the worst came to the worst, to come out on strike, giving due notice. They had no wish to undergo the hardships of unemployment or the rigours of the law, or to risk their meagre funds and imperil their friendly benefits, without good cause, and the typical 'craft' societies generally deplored mob violence. In non-craft trades, such as mining and cotton spinning, where the division between capital and labour was deepest and the feelings of exploitation keenest, violence was apt to flare up; but the histories even of these unions (which, with their relatively well-paid skilled workers, had 'aristocratic' attitudes similiar to those of the handicraft societies) are more consistently remarkable for their organised procedures and disciplined control.

The historian who has laid most emphasis on the class-revolutionary aspects of this early period has been Edward Thompson in his massive and intriguing study of *The Making of the English Working Class* (1963; Penguin ed., 1968) between the years 1780 and 1832. Although his main emphasis is on political and social developments, he frequently links these with trade unionism and he provides a superb, though brief, survey of the early craft societies in his chapter on 'Artisans and Others' (from which most of the following references are taken). Above all, he is concerned to demonstrate 'the making of the working class', 'the growth of class-consciousness: the consciousness of an identity of interests' on the part of English working people, against the middle and upper classes, against their employers and rulers. It is extremely difficult, however, to see in what ways this alleged class consciousness resulted in working-class solidarity or united action in that period, especially if one looks at the multitude of small sectional trade societies in London and provincial towns. Thompson himself emphasises the important point made above, that factory workers were a minority in this period and that the manufacturing population was composed mainly of handicraft workers in traditional trades such as handloom weaving, tailoring, hatting, shoemaking, building, cabinet-making, printing, and a host of other trades. He also emphasises that among such workers not only was craft sectionalism extremely strong, but that there was an even deeper division between 'artisans and others', i.e. between skilled craftsmen and semi-skilled or unskilled workers or labourers. Working men, as he notes, were keenly aware of these differences. Francis Place, for example, deplored the upper-class tendency to lump all working people together as 'the lower orders', to class 'the most skilled and the most prudent workmen, with the most ignorant and imprudent labourers and paupers, though the difference is great indeed, and indeed in many cases will scarce admit of comparison'. Thompson also notes the early nineteenth-century use of the term 'aristocracy' with reference to skilled artisans. As he points out, it is a commonly held opinion 'that the phenomenon of a "labour aristocracy" was coincident with the skilled trade unionism of the 1850s and 1860s', i.e. with the so-called 'New Model' unions (see below, pp. 20–1, 47, 50–5). But Thompson clearly shows that the Webbs were right in their analysis of trade-society origins: that these 'labour aristocratic' features were deeply rooted in the organisation and policies of the early craft societies. In such artisan trades, the gulf between the skilled (usually apprenticed) journeymen and labourers was deeper, psychologically and sometimes economically, than between themselves and small masters. There was even, as he points out, a higher aristocracy, composed of the most skilled and highly paid trades, *within* the labour aristocracy. This aristocratic outlook in the older trades, moreover, was also characteristic of the new elite of skilled workers in the iron, engineering and cotton manufactures in the late eighteenth and early nineteenth centuries.

Thompson also points out that there was already a strong tendency, early in the nineteenth century, as exemplified particularly in Francis Place, for politically-conscious skilled workers to collaborate with middle-class or aristocratic reformers. This was 'the policy of those self-respecting tradesmen or artisans who preferred to build bridges towards the middle class than to try and bridge the gulf between themselves and the tumultuous poor' ([16] 152–3). Indeed, much of their effort was concentrated on keeping out the poor – the 'unlawful', unapprenticed, semi-skilled workers – from their own jealously guarded trades, so as to maintain their status, employment and wages in a rapidly changing industrial world. At the same time, as the Webbs emphasised, 'industrial society [was] still divided trade by trade, instead of horizontally between employers and wage-earners', and craftsmen fought to maintain these demarcation lines against interlopers from other trades, as well as from below ([36] 45–6).

Membership of these trade societies was usually very small. 'Some of the trade clubs in 1825 had fewer than 100 members, and not many exceeded 500' ([16] 264). They were mostly local, restricted to members of a particular craft in a particular town, but, as the Webbs pointed out, there were signs of wider, even national, organisation in some trades, such as the hatters. Thompson quotes contemporary evidence to show how, in the early nineteenth century, the London shoemakers' society kept up 'a well-regulated correspondence with the trade in every city and town, of any importance, throughout the kingdom'. Similar links were formed between local societies in the printing trade, encouraged particularly by the system of tramp relief for unemployed members [65] 15, 29–30). Woolcombers and shearmen appear to have established national unions, though perhaps not permanently ([22] 57). Handloom weavers in the cotton industry formed wider federations from the end of the eighteenth century, and the new factory mule-spinners similarly combined in large-scale wages movements in 1810 and 1818 ([71] 62–70).

For the most part, however, trade societies were local, sectional and small-scale, based on public houses, or 'houses of call'. Moreover, society members – the 'honourable' part of the trade – were usually only a small proportion of the total number employed in it. As apprenticeship regulations and trade-union defences tended to crumble under the pressure of technological innovation, growing population and unemployment, the number of 'dishonourables' (non-society men, 'illegal' or non-apprenticed workers, those working below society wage-rates) tended to grow. Thompson refers to Mayhew's estimate in the mid-nineteenth century that 'as a general rule . . . the society-men of every trade comprise about one-tenth of the whole', although the evidence which Mayhew adduces suggests that the proportion was probably one-fifth or one-sixth ([16] 227). As Thompson points out, there is a tendency to exaggerate the prosperity of the skilled artisans, under such economic and social pressures, by referring to figures of wage-rates. There is certainly evidence in the printing trade, for example ([65] 24–5, 42–56), that skilled artisans were not always so well off as Clapham, Ashton and Chaloner have argued.

There is no doubt, however, that skilled artisans were *relatively* prosperous, compared with the mass of unskilled workers and labourers at or near subsistence level. They were also able to protect themselves to some extent in times of difficulty, and to preserve their 'respectability', by means of their friendly benefits. These, often mistakenly associated only with the later so-called 'New Model' unions, were in fact widespread from the earliest origins of trade societies. Such mutual support in times of unemployment, sickness and death, and sometimes also in old age, was as important to the members as more purely 'trade' matters such as wages, hours and apprenticeship. At the same time, friendly-society functions were often a cover for trade-union activity. This 'mutuality' or 'brotherhood', together with the close and secretive, but democratic, procedures typical of these small trade clubs, can be most vividly recaptured in that curiously fascinating book by Kiddier on *The Old Trade Unions* (1930), as exemplified in the minute-books and accounts of the brushmakers' society.

Another distinguishing feature of these skilled artisans was their general literacy. Many had some schooling, while others performed feats of self-education. Some were secular and rationalist in outlook, deriving their ideas from Paine or Owen, but others (especially in the provinces) were strongly influenced by Methodism, as Wearmouth has shown [18], and as Hobsbawm has emphasised ([12] chap. 3). The 'Primitives' particularly, with their lay preachers and democratic spirit, provided experience in public speaking, 'missionary' work and corporate organisation. The emotional, millenarian aspects of Methodism, on the other hand, were more likely to appear among less educated agricultural labourers, miners, etc., rather than among artisans.

Thompson, like the Webbs, emphasises the continuity in trade-union traditions and organisation. But the deeply-rooted sectionalism and aristocratic exclusiveness, which formed the basis of trade unionism throughout the first three-quarters of the nineteenth century, hardly squares with his emphasis on the full development of class consciousness. There were certainly signs that class consciousness was emerging, as Briggs had previously observed ([8] chap 1), and it is evident in the mutual assistance given by numerous trade societies to others involved in strikes, in the general opposition to the Combination Laws, as well as in expressions of solidarity to be found in such trade-union organs as the *Trades' Newspaper* of the mid-1820s or the *Voice of the People* in the early 1830s. Even in so 'aristocratic' a trade as the printers, it has been found that – contrasting with their generally sectional and exclusive attitude – there are signs that 'as the printing industry developed and capitalist competition grew, as the old gild regulations decayed and the influx of [excessive numbers of] apprentices broke down the barriers of exclusiveness, printers began to feel their interests at one with those of other workers whose customary standard of life was threatened by the same economic forces. Thus there is visible among them a growing solidarity with other sections of the "proletariat" ' ([65] 76). But although a general class consciousness was beginning to emerge, it was very shallow and vague, and the basic sectional and 'aristocratic' interests were usually predominant. For this reason, as Thompson recognises, 'many writers prefer the term working *classes*, which emphasizes the great disparity in status, acquisitions, skills, conditions, within the portmanteau phrase' ([16] 212). These disparities continued to exist, indeed, long after 1832, as

Thompson himself is aware: 'The distinction between the artisan and the labourer – in terms of status, organization, and economic reward – remained as great, if not greater, in Henry Mayhew's London of the late 1840s and 1850s as it was during the Napoleonic Wars' ([16] 266). Mayhew spoke of the transition from the skilled West End tradesmen to the unskilled East End labourers as like going into 'a new land, and among another race'.

For these reasons, Pelling rightly maintains that it is 'a mistake . . . to speak of a homogeneous "working class" in Britain at any time before the later nineteenth century' ([33] 4–6). Neale has emphasised the need for more refined sociological analysis, suggesting five classes instead of three, with a 'middling' class in the centre, composed of the upper working and lower middle classes, clearly differentiated from the proletarians at the bottom [97]. Hobsbawm has also emphasised the division between the 'labour aristocracy' and the labouring poor, but he has made some curiously conflicting statements on this subject [12] chap. 15). He argues that a true 'labour aristocracy' (associated with 'New Model' unionism) existed only from the 1840s onwards. Referring to the preceding period, he states that 'it is very doubtful whether in this period we can speak of a labour aristocracy at all', though its elements existed. Indeed, quite contrary to Thompson, he doubts 'whether we can speak of a proletariat in the developed sense at all, for this class was still in the process of emerging from the mass of petty producers, small masters, countrymen, etc., of pre-industrial society', though he recognises that 'in certain regions and industries it had already taken fairly definite shape'. He tends to evade the fact that even in 'pre-industrial' handicraft trades there had long been a considerable number of artisan wage-earners, who had formed the earliest trade societies and who remained among the most strongly organised far into the nineteenth century, making up a substantial proportion of the 'labour aristocracy'. He admits that in this early period 'we can, of course, establish individual categories of workers who can be regarded as labour aristocrats, and who showed the typical conservatism and sectional exclusiveness of their type', e.g. printers, engineers, ironfounders, and various other craftsmen. But he tends greatly to minimise the number of such skilled, comparatively well-off artisans, and thinks it best not to separate them 'from the rest of the labouring poor'. For Hobsbawm, in fact, a true 'proletariat' only emerges in the period after the 1840s, with increasingly large-scale capitalist organisation, but this he links questionably with the rise of a 'labour aristocracy'. At the same time, however, he recognises, even in this later period, the widespread survival of small-scale handicraft production, and in analysing the trade-union movement in 1875 he concedes that 'somewhat more than half of it was made up of craftsmen in trades little affected . . . by the industrial revolution', including many traditional crafts. 'We may note', he adds, 'that a list compiled for the first half of the century would not have read very differently.' And later he remarks that the labour aristocracy 'was probably no larger in the 1860s and 1870s than the favoured strata had been before 1850'.

3 *Repeal of the Combination Laws*

ONE of the most deeply-rooted myths in trade-union history is that of the cruelly oppressive Combination Laws. This belief, however, is based on historical error and misconception. It arises mainly from confusion of the Combination Laws of 1799–1800 with other, older, legal controls, which were actually more severe and more frequently enforced.

From their earliest days, trade societies had been subject to legal repression. Under common law they were illegal 'conspiracies' acting 'in restraint of trade'. Under the Elizabethan Statute of Artificers (1563) trade unionists could be punished for leaving work unfinished (as in a strike), and they could also be penalised under the law of contract relating to 'master and servant'. During the eighteenth century, moreover, many Acts against 'combinations' were procured by employers in particular trades. Thus long before the Combination Acts were passed, there was a formidable legal armoury which could be used against trade societies. On the other hand, it should not be supposed that these laws were constantly and ruthlessly applied; in fact, they were only enforced sporadically, and, as we have seen, innumerable trade societies had sprung into existence during the eighteenth century. There is no doubt, however, that the laws relating to such 'combinations' were unjustly one-sided, an example of 'class' legislation; although employers' associations to control prices and wages were also illegal at common law, they were very rarely prosecuted.

To what extent, then, did the Combination Laws of 1799–1800 constitute a new departure, and what were their effects? The Webbs described them as a 'far-reaching change of policy' by Parliament, under the shadow of the French Revolution and fear of working-class conspiracies. Although there had been previous Acts dealing with combinations in particular trades, the 1799 Act was the first general statutory prohibition of *all* combinations. It was partly inspired by fears of revolution, but was also intended 'to stop obstructions to trade which were intolerable in war-time and were in fact illegal' ([26] 177); industrial dislocation and inflation during the war, of course, increased social unrest. This Act, which applied only to combinations of workmen, was mainly intended to secure speedy settlement of disputes by summary proceedings before a single magistrate. It provided penalties of up to three months' imprisonment (two with hard labour) for trade-union activities in regard to wages and hours. It was passed through Parliament with little discussion and without attracting much notice. It soon led, however, to protests against its unfairness and was repealed by an Act of the following year, which laid down modified controls. Two justices were now required, and they must not be masters in the trade concerned; only offences 'maliciously and wilfully' committed could be penalised; arbitration clauses were introduced (though they never seem to have been operated); and the Act applied to employers as well as workmen (a section that proved equally inoperative).

Was this legislation, as the Webbs call it, 'a new and momentous departure'? The researches of Dorothy George [25, 26], subsequently supported by those of Aspinall [1], have shown convincingly that it was *not*: that, in fact, it 'represented no change of policy', that it 'merely added one more to the many existing Statutes'. True, it was general instead of particular legislation, but it contained no new principle, nor was it distinguished from earlier laws by its severity – in fact the penalties were considerably lighter than those which could be imposed under common law prosecutions. Moreover, its effects have been greatly exaggerated. The Act was not very frequently used, and when used was often ineffective; its main intention (summary jurisdiction) was largely defeated by appeals to the Sessions and the frequent quashing of convictions on technical points. Thus the 1800 Act 'was in practice a very negligible instrument of oppression'. Employers continued to rely mainly on the older legal controls provided by common law, the Statute of Artificers, and the law of master and servant.

There is no doubt that workmen's combinations were subjected to legal persecution during the early nineteenth century. There are many examples of prosecutions, fines and imprisonment. Repression appears to have been worst in the areas of most rapid technological change, or where outwork was extensive, and where, therefore, class differences were becoming more pronounced, as in the textile districts of Lancashire and Nottinghamshire, where combinations tended to be most violent, with machine-breaking, etc. But in older, skilled handicrafts, although there were some prosecutions, trade societies were generally recognised by employers and often negotiated openly for increased wages, etc. In the evidence before the Select Committee on Artisans and Machinery in 1824, there were many examples of tolerance and compromise: many employers did not choose to take legal proceedings, but preferred collective bargaining, either because they wished to preserve good feeling, or because of the effects of strikes on their business, or through fear of violence, or because of the expenses and uncertainties of the law. George White, clerk to this Committee and very knowledgeable on the subject, stated that the Combination Act of 1800 had 'been in general a dead letter upon those artisans upon whom it was intended to have an effect; namely, the shoemakers, printers, papermakers, shipbuilders, tailors, etc., who have had their regular societies and houses of call, as though no such Act was in existence'.

Despite all this overwhelming weight of evidence, however, the legend regarding the Combination Laws is still kept alive. Thompson, for example, declares that Dr George's general interpretation is 'untrue', although he admits almost all the points she has produced; he recognises that the chief novelty of the Combination Laws was simply their general prohibition, that no new legal principle was involved, and that there is no truth in the popular belief 'that the Combination Acts made illegal trade unions which were legal before', because there were already various legal means of prosecuting trade

Unions ([16] chap. 13, sec. iii). He states that the Combination Laws 'were often employed', though 'no count has been made of the number of cases brought under them'; 'no one familiar with these years can doubt that their general prohibitive influence was ever-present', yet 'they were not as widely employed as might have been expected', and 'employers were often reluctant to use the Acts as more than a threat'. In many trades, especially the skilled handicrafts, 'trade-union activity was still, in practice, accepted as permissible', but outside these artisan trades, in the manufacturing districts of the Midlands, North and West, 'repression of trade unionism was very much more severe'; yet 'even here the Combination Acts were not always brought into use . . . prosecutions often took place, not under the Acts of 1799–1800, but under previous legislation'. Trade societies were constantly repressed, yet there is 'the paradox that . . . in the years when the Acts were in force . . . trade unionism registered great advances', that during these years not only did long-established trade societies 'continue more or less unperturbed', but trade unionism spread to many new trades and there were even the first attempts at general union.

Thompson perpetuates the very confusion which Dr George pointed out was mainly responsible for the creation of the erroneous myth of the Combination Laws: 'that these were the only Acts styled Combination Acts, and therefore all the opprobrium attaching to the mass of legislation repealed in 1824 was loosely and vaguely attached to the Act of 1800' ([26] 176–7). Witnesses before the 1824 Committee were confused as to whether prosecutions had been brought under the Combination Law, or for common law conspiracy, for riot, for assault, or for breach of contract, or for leaving work unfinished. Thompson therefore argued that 'from the point of view of the trade unionists, it made little difference whether they were prosecuted under the [Combination] Acts, or under common law or 5 Eliz. c.4, except that the latter were more severe or more expeditious. To the general public, in any case, *all* this legislation was grouped under the generic term, "the laws against combination". . . . Under one law or another, blows were struck at the unionists. . . .'

These statements are undoubtedly true – that is indeed how 'the Combination Laws' appeared to contemporary trade unionists. But though it may have 'made little difference' to them which law was utilised against them, it certainly does make a difference to a correct historical appreciation of whether or not the Combination Laws marked 'a new and momentous departure' and as to whether or not they made legal repression more severe. Other left-wing writers have accepted Dr George's evidence. Allen, for example, agrees that the Webbs' account 'over-emphasises the significance of the Combination Acts. There were other more repressive measures against trade unions which employers in the main preferred to use. The Acts did little more than signify a state of mind influenced by the French Revolution' ([19] 5). About all that can be said in support of the legend is, as Thompson rightly says, that they exercised a 'general deterrent influence': even though not often invoked, they could, as Dr George pointed out, be 'used *in terrorem* to stop strikes'.

Thompson also supports what the Webbs called the 'romantic legend' of secret meetings, hidden records, awe-inspiring oaths and initiation ceremonies, during these years of trade-union repression ([36] 64). There is no doubt something in this legend, but there is also a mass of evidence to show that many trade societies existed and negotiated with employers quite openly. Connected with this legend is another: that (in Thompson's words) there was 'a widespread, secret combination', half political ('Jacobin'), half industrial (trade unionist); the Combination Acts 'brought the Jacobin tradition into association with the illegal unions'. But the evidence which Thompson produces for such widespread revolutionary trade unionism is extremely thin and exaggerated (as such rumours were apt to be at the time). The vast majority of references in the Home Office papers produced by Aspinall, by contrast, are concerned with combinations and strikes about wages, 'illegal' men, apprentices, machinery, and other purely 'trade' affairs [1]. Thompson himself has to warn that 'we must not paint too colourful a picture of the heroic days of illegality'.

The campaign for repeal of the Combination Laws, conducted by Francis Place, is well known from the Webbs' *History*. Thompson, while accepting this account in the main, makes some valid reinterpretative comments. He points out that Place – a devotee of orthodox 'political economy', an advocate of *laissez-faire* and freedom of contract, who thought that repeal of the Combination Laws would bring trade unionism and strikes to an end – was, not surprisingly, distrusted by many trade unionists, and that it was this caution, rather than 'apathy' (as alleged by the Webbs), that caused them to be lukewarm at first in their support. Thompson also points out that Place was not conducting an entirely single-handed campaign. Nevertheless, he was 'the main architect of repeal', though Thompson is obviously reluctant to make this concession to such a doctrinaire supporter of 'political economy' and such 'a great wire-puller'. Moreover, Thompson states that 'except in certain craft unions' – a large exception – trade unionists did not accept Place's advocacy of 'class collaboration' and that repeal of the Combination Laws led immediately to class warfare by trade unionists and Owenite socialists. In fact, however, as Thompson himself recognises elsewhere, there was a strong tradition of class collaboration (see above, pp. 16–17 which was soon to be demonstrated during the Reform Bill agitation; and Owenite socialism was not an expression of class hostility, for Owen's philosophy was essentially class-collaborationist (see below, p. 33).

The 1824 Act not only swept away the Combination Laws, but also excluded trade unions from prosecution for conspiracy, etc., under common or statute law. Trade societies, therefore, at once 'sprang into existence or emerged into aggressive publicity on all sides' ([36] 104). With trade booming, there were numerous movements for wage increases, accompanied by strikes and violence. The result was an immediate demand by employers for reimposition of the Combination Laws, and it required all Place's diplomacy, backed by strong trade-union protests, to prevent this, after appointment of another Committee. The repealing Act of 1825 was, in fact, a compromise: the rights of combination and collective bargaining on wages and hours were maintained, but trade societies were again made subject to the common law of conspiracy to prevent criminal acts of intimidation and coercion. This Act is rightly regarded as a milestone in trade-union history, but there was still a long way to go to secure legal status and freedom. In fact, numerous prosecutions of trade unionists continued to occur in the following years, under common law or the law of master and servant, or under more obscure legislation such as that against illegal oaths utilised against the 'Tolpuddle Martyrs'.

4 *The Era of Doherty and Owen*

DURING the years after 1825, trade societies of the traditional 'craft' type and of the newer elite of cotton spinners and engineers continued to pursue much the same practical policies as in the past, despite wider but ephemeral excitements. The Webbs, however, in their *History,* highlighted those developments, such as Owenite socialism, which they (as Fabian socialists) considered especially significant, while they dealt inadequately with the more purely 'trade' aspects. There is, however, plenty of evidence, especially in trade-union records (where these have survived), to indicate that the latter constituted the most essential, solid and continuous features of trade unionism in the nineteenth century, i.e. patient organisation, collective bargaining on wages, hours, apprentices and working conditions, and arrangement of friendly benefits for unemployment, sickness and death. The practical effects of ideology – whether of Owenite socialism in this period, or of classical economics later – upon the actual organisation and policies of most trade societies appear to have been very superficial, and were greatly exaggerated in importance by the Webbs. This was not, on the whole, a 'revolutionary' period in trade-union history [19, 31].

Nevertheless, there were significant developments during these years, though certainly not so novel or sweeping as generally believed. The first were organisational: the formation of more district and national unions, and even attempts at general trades' union or federation. The second were ideological: the broadening of trade-union horizons to include political and social ideas, Radical and Owenite-socialist. These two lines of development tended to become associated, most notably in Owen's Grand National Consolidated Trades Union, but they were never successfully welded together, and trade unions in general held aloof from the Radical and socialist movements. (For Radicalism, see below, pp. 36–48.)

The outburst of trade-union activity during the years 1829–34 was not, as is so often imagined, dominated by Owenite-socialist enthusiasm. It was, in fact, a mainly endogenous trade-union movement, encouraged psychologically if not legally by the repeal of the Combination Laws. The formation of district and national unions was not new (see above, p. 17). In 1818–19, moreover, there had even been an attempt at general union, the 'Philanthropic Society', or 'Philanthropic Hercules', for the purpose of raising a strike fund ([1] 272–4; [22] 8–11; [36] 114). The practical aims were also unaltered: to fight against wage reductions, the breakdown of apprenticeship regulations and heavy unemployment. The cotton spinners, for example, in organising their Grand General Union in 1829 – preceded by similar general movements in 1810 and 1825 – were motivated by purely trade-union aims regarding wages, entry to the trade and establishment of a strike fund. So too were the letterpress printers in establishing their Northern Union in 1830; organisation of tramp relief for the unemployed was also a strong motive. The same is true of the miners, builders, potters and other workers who began to organise wider district or national unions during these years. These unions in particular trades, pursuing bread-and-butter objectives, were of much greater practical significance, though less grandiose and ambitious, than attempts at 'general union' during these years. The future was to be with them, rather than in vast trades' federations – especially of the utopian Owenite type – which have never proved successful in this country. Whereas the general unions soon collapsed, the sectional ones, though weakened by strikes and lock-outs, in most cases survived or were soon resuscitated.

Many trade societies, it is true, were influenced by Owenite ideas. A small minority of idealists wrote and spoke in favour of general union and a co-operative–socialist millennium, but the effects of their propaganda on trade societies has been grossly exaggerated. Most trade societies, in fact, were not prepared to subordinate their autonomy or their traditional policies to Owen's 'new view of society', though they might express some sympathy with his aims. A few started small schemes of co-operative production, but mostly as a means of relieving unemployed or striking members rather than as serious attempts at altering the social system. There was, in fact, much trade-union criticism of the impracticable aspects of Owenite co-operative schemes. The National Association for the Protection of Labour – an attempt at general union or trades' federation – was in no sense an Owenite body, but grew out of the failure of the Lancashire cotton spinners' strike in 1829 and was primarily an attempt at organising a general strike fund. This above all is what attracted other trade societies into it, though it did provide wider social and political horizons, especially in its journal, the *Voice of the People,* edited by John Doherty. Most affiliated societies, however, were primarily concerned with their sectional trade objectives, and it collapsed with the failure of numerous piecemeal strikes.

G. D. H. Cole's account of the general movements of these years [22] is inaccurate on a number of important points. John Doherty, for example, as current research will show, was not really an Owenite socialist; he always put practical trade-union objectives first, and although he certainly expressed approval of 'this beautiful system' (Owenite co-operation), there is no evidence that he became actively involved in it, or that he tried to divert either the cotton spinners' trade union or the National Association into such millenarian or utopian schemes, as he is said to have done by Cole, followed uncritically by other writers such as Morris, Thompson, Turner and Rudé. Similarly, although it is true that he wrote and spoke strongly in favour of political reform, it is not generally realised that his growing involvement in Radical and other movements aroused strong opposition among the cotton spinners, with the result that he was soon removed or resigned from the secretaryship of the Manchester society, the spinners' General Union, and the National Association. He set up a printing and bookselling business and involved himself in Radical journalism, as well as in the factory reform movement, and tended to drift out of the main stream of active trade unionism. His association with Owen and Fielden in the 'Society for National Regeneration' of 1833 was, despite the high-sounding title, really part of the 'short-time' movement, to which the spinners turned after their disastrous failures in 1829–30, a natural trade-union reaction in a period of depression and unemployment; but this general movement, like the earlier ones, quickly collapsed from lack of widespread support. Moreover, the spinners held aloof from Owen's 'Grand National' in 1834. In fact, as Turner has shown, the predominant feature of the spinners' trade societies during these years was their strongly sectional and local characteristics; it proved impossible to organise a successful national spinners' union, and their support for general trades' union was even weaker.

The same is true of similar movements in other trades. The builders, for example, though briefly penetrated by co-operative–socialist ideas, were also too sectional and localised for attempted general union to be successful. Moreover, the basic interests that briefly united them in the Operative Builders' Union were concerned with such purely 'trade' affairs as 'the contracting system', wages and apprentices; Morrison's syndicalist schemes, as expounded in the *Pioneer,* quickly foundered, and there was a reversion to the sectional 'craft' organisations of stonemasons, carpenters, etc.

Regional separatism is visible in the Yorkshire 'Trades Union' (mainly in the woollen and worsted trades, but including various others). Cole has shown that this was not, as the Webbs stated, part of Doherty's National Association; it was mainly concerned with trying to establish a uniform scale of wages, and at first seemed to enjoy some success, but it too ended in strike failures in 1833–4. Even less ambitious district unions in particular trades, such as that of the Northumberland and Durham miners, organised in the early 1830s, experienced similar failures when faced by the combined opposition of employers.

Owen's Grand National Consolidated Trades Union brought this ferment in trade unionism to its greatest height, and to its end. It was, in fact, mainly a revival of

Doherty's earlier general union, and although it is one of the most famous phenomena in nineteenth-century trade unionism – associated with one of the most fascinating figures in labour history, Robert Owen, and also with possibly the most famous episode (apart from the General Strike of 1926), that of the 'Tolpuddle Martyrs' – it must be emphasised that it was even less successful than the National Association, that it lasted for only a year, that it never became the vast organisation into which it was inflated by the Webbs, and that it proved a complete failure. Robert Owen was never really interested in trade unions as such; he regarded them as futile and hoped to convert them to his schemes of co-operative socialism. His utopian, pacifist ideas, however, were unacceptable to most trade unionists, who were more interested in a general union for supporting strikes. On the other hand, the extreme militant plan for a 'grand national holiday', or general strike, quite contrary to Owen's philosophy, also failed to win any widespread support. The Webbs' figure of half a million members in the G.N.C.T.U. has been shown by Oliver to be ridiculously inflated [99]. The total paid-up membership appears to have been only about 16,000, though a larger penumbra may have been vaguely connected with it; the Union failed to attract the vast majority of trade societies – the London tailors, shoemakers and silk-weavers, in fact, formed the greater part of it. Most of the skilled societies, such as those of the cotton spinners, builders, engineers and printers, held aloof, and although a few labourers (like those at Tolpuddle) were briefly organised, unionism spread to only a very limited extent beyond the traditional craft boundaries. It had no solid organisation or finances, and it collapsed like a balloon in the face of employers' lock-outs and prosecutions, including, of course, that of the wretched 'Dorchester labourers'. It was a fascinating phenomenon, but sadly ephemeral.

No doubt it will continue to fascinate all who are interested in labour history. It has an element of drama about it: it rises above the limited, practical, mundane concerns of sectional craft societies, providing apocalyptic visions of a non-competitive co-operative society and the brotherhood of man – only to collapse miserably and disappear. Thompson still considers that the attempts at general union in the early 1830s expressed working-class consciousness 'on an unprecedented scale' ([16] 887–8). He still maintains, moreover, that the 'Grand National' demonstrated the triumph of industrial-syndicalist ideas: 'When Marx was still in his teens, the battle for the minds of English trade unionists, between a capitalist and a socialist political economy, had been (at least temporarily) won.' He admits, however, that 'this vision was lost, almost as soon as it had been found' ([16] 912–13). It was, in fact, a vision which appeared to only a small minority of trade unionists and which never materialised. The 'Grand National', as other modern left-wing historians now recognise, 'was not an Owenite body but one intended to organize efficient strike relief' ([103] 207), and even in that more limited aim it proved an utter failure.

Unfortunately, however, the Webbs' inflation of the Owenite episode in 1833–4 caused them to produce a warped interpretation of subsequent trade-union development. There was not such a catastrophic collapse after 1834 as they suggest; in fact, most of the traditionally organised craft societies remained in existence, either in local trade clubs or in loose federal unions. The Webbs' wild guess of half a million members in the G.N.C.T.U., however, contrasted with their estimate of less than 100,000 trade unionists in the late 1830s, creates an extremely misleading impression. Moreover, to account for the apparent change in trade-union organisation and philosophy in the later period, they had, as we shall see, to create a mythical 'New Model' of trade unionism (see below, pp. 50–2).

The history of trade unionism in the later 1830s and early 1840s has been inadequately investigated, but there is abundant evidence in the Report of the Select Committee on Combinations in 1838, and also in local newspapers and surviving, though scrappy, trade-union records, to indicate that a large number of societies remained in existence after 1834. They had to face great difficulties between 1836 and 1842 because of serious trade depression: the burden of unemployment, wage reductions and loss of membership may have caused some societies to collapse, but most of them appear to have survived. These, of course, were of the sectional, skilled type – unskilled labourers still remained almost entirely unorganised – and there was no change in the character of trade unionism during these years; when trade revived and the forward movement among trade unions was resumed in the 1840s, it was along the old lines.

5 *Trade Societies, Politics and the Trade Cycle*

IN early trade-union development, there was a strong tradition of looking to the State for protection. Trade societies had, for example, frequently petitioned Parliament for enforcement of the Elizabethan regulations regarding wages and apprenticeship. But during the eighteenth century Parliament, Government and local justices came increasingly to adopt a policy of *laissez-faire,* or non-interference in industrial affairs, and the ancient wages and apprenticeship clauses of the Statute of Artificers were finally abolished in 1813–14. Moreover, with the passing of the Combination Laws, Parliament was clearly coming down more heavily on the side of the employers. At the same time the ideas of the French Revolution, as expressed in this country in Paine's *Rights of Man,* began to exercise a powerful influence on the minds of politically-conscious working men and caused them to turn to Radicalism; the speeches and writings of Thelwall and Spence extended these ideas to include economic and social as well as political rights.

Thompson has described very vividly how these ideas mingled with the older Radical traditions of urban artisans and tradesmen and were further stimulated by the economic and social effects of the Industrial Revolution, to produce the Radical movement of the London Corresponding Society and similar societies in other towns, and how the movement survived repression and revived in the later years of the war to become a mass movement after 1815, when a spur was given to Radicalism by post-war economic depression. Thompson has tended, however, to exaggerate the extent to which this was a working-class movement. Radicalism was middle- as well as working-class, and even attracted some upper-class support. Most of the main leaders, in fact, were middle-class, or had risen from the working classes into the lower middle class: Paine, Thelwall, Spence, Hardy, Cartwright, Place, Hunt, Cobbett – these were not horny-handed sons of toil, any more than, say, Owen and Thompson in the later co-operative movement, O'Brien and O'Connor in Chartism, or Marx and Engels in revolutionary socialism. Other, less doctrinaire, labour historians, such as Briggs, though well aware of the growth of class consciousness, have emphasised also the importance of class collaboration in the political reform movement. Indeed, Thompson himself, in many passages of his book (see, for example, [16] 22–3, 104–5, 152–3, 170–2), recognises that the social composition of this Radical movement was a mixture of classes, that there was a strong and long-continued tradition of class collaboration, with a predominantly non-socialist ideology, in favour of maintaining property rights and against economic levelling, and that the movement might therefore more properly be termed 'popular Radical' rather than 'working-class'.

Thompson also appears to have exaggerated the extent to which there was a merging of 'Jacobinism' and trade unionism during the war and post-war periods (see above, p. 26). There is, in fact, only vague and inadequate evidence on the political role of trade societies during those years. There is no doubt, of course, that large numbers of working men attended meetings and took part in demonstrations, though far fewer probably belonged to Radical societies. But to what extent trade societies *as such* – as distinct from individual members – actually took corporate political action is very doubtful.

This is equally true of the Radical agitation over the Reform Bill in the early 1830s. There simply is not enough evidence to be dogmatic on this point, but such evidence as there is tends to suggest that trade societies did not generally involve themselves in politics, though many of their members certainly were Radicals as well as trade unionists. There was a strong sentiment that trade unionism was one thing, politics another, and that trade societies should confine themselves to trade affairs, unless politics obviously impinged upon them, as in the case of the Combination Acts.

Other left-wing historians, however, have, like Thompson,

tried to demonstrate the essential solidarity of working-class movements in this period. Many have adopted a 'swing of the pendulum' theory of alternations from one kind of action to another, and this has tended to become a widespread assumption. Prothero, for example, asserts that 'it is common ground that working-class activity oscillated according to economic conditions, political agitation being more likely in bad times and trade unionism in good' ([103] 204). He bases this statement on Briggs' observation – that 'the pendulum swung between economic action through trade unions and political action through Chartism. "Good times" favoured the former: "bad times" the latter' ([86] 6) – and on Hobsbawm's investigation into the effects of the trade cycle on working-class movements (see below, p. 39).

There is some truth in this observation, but, as Prothero points out, it needs refinement (see below, p. 42), for his revised interpretation). It is very doubtful, for example, whether there were any large-scale desertions from trade unions into politics, and vice versa, according to the state of trade. It is often said, however, that swings occurred according to disillusionment first with one and then with the other. Thus, in the years 1830–2, it is said, working-class activity swung away from trade unionism into politics, after failure of strikes in 1829–30; but then disillusionment with the Reform Bill caused a swing back into trade unionism combined with Owenite socialism; after the collapse of the 'Grand National' in 1834, however, there was a gradual swing back to Radical activity, leading to Chartism; but again, when Chartism failed in the late 1830s and early 1840s, there was a revival of trade unionism in the middle 1840s, only to be followed by a swing back to Chartism again in 1847–8; and after the Chartist collapse in 1848, there came 'New Model' trade unionism.

This pendulum theory is often associated with the trade cycle, as evidenced by the statements of Briggs and Prothero. That trade fluctuations had profound social effects is, of course, generally agreed: changes in the level of industrial and commercial activity obviously affected employment, wages and the cost of living, and the resultant pattern of prosperity and depression, it would seem equally obvious, must have been closely related to trade-union and other working-class movements. But this relationship was more complex than is often realised, and has never, in fact, been adequately investigated. There are, however, good grounds for suggesting that 'the trade cycle had much more effect on trade-union development in the nineteenth century than the ideological fluctuations propounded by the Webbs' ([31] 7). Their division of trade-union history into a 'revolutionary period' (1829–42), followed by a 'new spirit' and 'new model' (1843–60), simply does not accord with the facts (see above, pp. 29–35, and below, pp. 49–58). The pattern of boom and slump, on the other hand, is certainly reflected in the ups and downs – and possibly also in the alternations – of trade-union and political activity. But the reflection is by no means clear and simple.

Hobsbawm was the first labour historian to examine this question with any seriousness ([12] chap. 8). The problem, he points out, arises mainly in the period before 1850: in the second half of the century there is a much clearer and more general relationship between the trade cycle and trade unionism, with growth of membership and forward movements for wage advances, etc., in booms, and falling-off in membership and defensive actions in slumps. In the earlier period, however, Hobsbawm lumps all working-class movements together, on grounds of class solidarity, without distinguishing between the trade-union, Owenite and political aspects; he considers that 'the sharp distinction between industrial and political action is . . . artificial', and that Owenism in the early 1830s and Chartism in the later 1830s made 'the very heterogeneous (and often contradictory) forces of discontent' into 'a single, however fragile, national force'. He follows Rostow's theory of harvest fluctuations – bad harvests in this period causing not only high food prices but also industrial slumps, wage-cuts and unemployment, an obviously explosive mixture. Thus before 1850 social movements were the result of 'catastrophic and simultaneous increases in misery for most of the working population. . . . Expansions occurred at or near the bottom of the slumps.'

This theory, however, is far too simplistic to fit the facts.

Indeed, Hobsbawm himself expresses serious doubts about it. He includes, for example, the years 1838–42 together with 1833–5 among trade-union 'explosions'; but while the latter period (in a trade revival) was certainly one of trade-union expansion, the former (in a slump), while remarkable for the upsurge of Chartism, witnessed trade-union contraction. Hobsbawm recognises, in fact, that 'even before 1850 trade-union expansion had . . . tended to occur in the upswing of booms, e.g. in 1792, 1818, 1824–5 and 1844–6'. This causes him to question whether the harvest theory can be applied; indeed, he states that 'the primacy of the genuine trade cycle is not in much doubt after 1815'. But he finally concludes contradictorily: 'Still, slump "explosion" remains the rule before 1850. . . .'

Most of this confusion would disappear by distinguishing between the trade-union and political movements. It can be argued much more plausibly that trade unions tended to expand and be more aggressive in booms, and to decline and become more defensive in slumps, while political activity followed the reverse pattern. Trade-union advances tended to occur in periods of full employment, when conditions were favourable, while political activity rose in slumps when heavy unemployment was inhibiting trade unionism. But this model is also too simple to fit the facts completely. It is clearly evident, for example, that whilst there was certainly a trade-union outburst in the boom of 1824–5, coincidental with the repeal of the Combination Laws, there was another outburst during the subsequent depression in 1829–30, e.g. the cotton spinners' general union and the National Association, and this trade-union activity continued unabated in the period 1830–2, also depressed years, at the same time as the political agitation over the Reform Bill. Thus both the trade cycle and the pendulum theories are contradicted for these years. Moreover, though disillusionment with the Reform Bill may have combined with trade recovery to stimulate trade unionism in 1833–4, culminating in the 'Grand National', the movement broke before the boom reached its height in 1835–6. After that date, the facts fit the trade cycle theory much better: slump in the late 1830s and early 1840s caused trade unionism to decline, while social distress was the main force behind Chartism; trade recovery in the mid-1840s brought trade-union revival and a decline of Chartism; the situation was reversed again after the economic crisis of 1846–7.

Thompson, as staunch an advocate of class solidarity as Hobsbawm, will have none of these 'swings', but is equally inconsistent ([16] 909–13). 'The line from 1832 to Chartism', he declares, 'is not a haphazard pendulum alternation of "political" and "economic" agitations but a direct progression, in which simultaneous and related movements converge towards a single point.' But almost immediately we are told that the middle-class Reform Bill resulted in 'rejection, by the working class, of all forms of political action' and 'the post-1832 swing to general unionism'. Then, after the trade-union defeats of 1834–5, 'the workers returned to the vote' and Chartism began. So perhaps, after all, there *is* something in the 'swings' theory!

Further refinement, however, has been suggested. Hobsbawm perceptively observed that reactions to trade fluctuations varied as between different sections of the working class, e.g. 'between the sections of workers who normally lived . . . under conditions of full employment, and those who normally lived in a glutted labour market' ([12] 129, 149 n. 9). The better-off artisans in favoured trades relied on their trade unions and were opposed to political Radicalism in the 1830s and 1840s; but workers in depressed trades could achieve little by trade-union action and sought salvation mainly in politics. Turner has formulated a similar theory ([71] 70–8), pointing out that while the aristocratic cotton spinners during these years were aggressive in boom periods, seeking wage advances, but avoided challenges in slumps, the wretched handloom weavers merely fought defensive actions against wage-cuts in slumps. This theory, however, does not completely fit the facts: it applies to the spinners in the booms of 1818 and 1824–5, but not for 1829–30, which Turner wrongly describes as years of recovery, with movements for wage advances, when in fact these were depressed years and the spinners were fighting against reductions. But they were active again in the boom of the mid-1830s, as evidenced by the great

Preston strike of 1836. The weavers, moreover, did generally fight defensively in depressions, though they were also active in the boom of 1824–5; after 1830, however, they were too weak to support much trade-union action and turned to politics.

Prothero has produced a variant of this model ([103] 204–5), differentiating between 'the older craft, artisan, and building trades, with their traditions and experience of organisation', on the one hand, and the 'newer occupations without such traditions or experience, such as factory workers', on the other – the former being most active in seeking improvements in wages, hours, etc., during booms, when conditions were favourable, the latter tending to strike against reductions during economic depressions, rather than for advances in better times. The examples which he provides to support this theory, however, are not very convincing. It is true that the cotton spinners (and the National Association which they dominated) did strike in 1829–30, against wage reductions, during a depression, but their more usual pattern, as Turner points out, was of strikes for advances in booms. On the other hand, the strikes in 1833–4 among building workers, tailors and shoemakers (the last two trades dominating the 'Grand National') were certainly in a period of trade recovery. Prothero goes on to argue that the 'Plug Plot' strikes in the slump of 1842 were 'among unorganised workers, many of them factory hands', while the boom of 1844–5 saw the creation of new national unions among older artisan trades such as shoemakers and tailors, and the formation of the National Association of United Trades. The 'Plug Plot' strikes, however, were certainly not by 'unorganised workers', but included some well-organised trades, such as cotton spinners, while the shoemakers and tailors and the N.A.U.T., as Prothero emphasises later on, were examples of weak and depressed, though old, artisan trades.

In the main body of his article, in fact, Prothero makes a very plausible distinction, like that made by Thompson and Turner, between the 'upper trades', skilled workers in favoured trades, such as printers and engineers, and the 'lower trades', those much less favourably situated in depressed and declining trades, such as shoemakers and tailors (see below, p. 46). It is this distinction – not that between older, traditional, well-organised craftsmen and newer, inexperienced, poorly organised factory workers – which carries conviction. The strongly organised trades included the new elite of factory-working cotton spinners and engineers, as well as the old elite craftsmen such as printers, bookbinders, etc., while many of the depressed trades included older traditional crafts such as shoemaking, tailoring and handloom weaving, mostly out-work.

What pattern, then, emerges from all this theorising? There is little support for ideologically determined swings. The trade cycle, on the other hand, seems generally to have had a dominating influence on both trade-union and political activity. In booms, the favoured and strongly organised trades, both the old and new elite, conducted advance movements, while even the depressed trades had a respite and tried to strengthen their organisation. In slumps, the stronger trade societies tended to be more quietly defensive, though sometimes having to fight strongly against wage-cuts, while the depressed trades struggled in much direr straits. This cyclical pattern in trade unionism continued into the second half of the nineteenth century; there was no great 'economic watershed', as postulated by Hobsbawm, around mid-century.

The political swings may also be fitted into this economically determined pattern. In general, these were much more marked among the weaker or unorganised trades, for whom politics appeared to offer some hope in trade depressions; the stronger trades tended to hold aloof from politics, in both boom and slump, relying more on trade-union action. This general political pattern, however, did not apply invariably. There was considerable variation, as Briggs has emphasised, according to the local economic and social background.

In London, as Beer showed long ago [7], there were certainly important links in the early 1830s between politics, Owenite socialism and trade unionism. It was from among the 'trades' that the early metropolitan co-operative movement developed, metamorphosing first into the Metropolitan Trades Union and then into the politically orientated National Union of the Working Classes. It is by no means clear, however, how widely and actively London trade societies participated in the Reform Bill agitation, or to what extent this agitation was on a 'class' basis. Thompson quotes Place's reference to reform meetings held 'by journeymen tradesmen in their clubs' ([16] 889), and evidence from the brushmakers' records shows them subscribing to reform associations ([36] 177); but neither Briggs nor Rowe in their studies of the London movement have produced evidence of actual trade-society involvement.[1] Briggs notes that certain superior craftsmen, such as the engineers, held aloof from politics, but that a minority, including Lovett, Hetherington and others, provided Radical leadership ([86] 4–5). As Thompson recognises, however, it is 'problematical' how far these militant Radicals 'represented any massive body of working-class opinion' ([16] 893). Many moderate working-class Radicals in London favoured Place's policy of co-operation with the middle classes to secure the Reform Bill. Class divisions were not clearly defined in the numerous small-scale metropolitan trades, and both middle and working classes combined in the National Political Union.

In Birmingham similarly, there was generally class co-operation in the Political Union, because social differences between small masters and skilled artisans were blurred in the metals manufactures. In Manchester, on the other hand, where social divisions were deeper, with the growth of the factory system, there was much more class feeling and hostility, expressed fiercely in the separate Workmen's Union, but how far this was supported by the trade societies is doubtful. Doherty was certainly a staunch Radical, but by the early 1830s he had ceased to hold an official position in the spinners' union; his wider political and social activities had aroused strong opposition (see above, p. 31). Turner says nothing of any political action by spinners or handloom weavers in the Reform Bill crisis, though he makes several references to the weavers' strong Radical tradition. (As a depressed section, they were much more politically inclined than

[1] A. Briggs, *Cambridge Historical Journal,* x 3 (1952); D. J. Rowe, *Historical Journal,* xiii 1 (1970).

the spinners.) Rudé points out the influence of the French Revolution during the 1830 cotton spinners' strikes, the display of tricolour flags, and the authorities' fears of revolutionary outbreaks; but he considers that the factory workers 'were not yet ready to play an independent political role' [106]. The strike failures of 1829–30 greatly weakened their trade societies 'and they contributed comparatively little to the Reform movement of 1831'. Indeed, Rudé considers that, in general, trade unionism and political reform were at this time 'separate movements with their own distinctive aims and modes of conduct'.

In Leeds also, there was a division between trade unionism and Radicalism. Working-class Radicals, so Briggs informs us, supported a political programme based on universal suffrage rather than an economic programme based on strikes and machine-breaking, because to build trade unions was (according to the *Leeds Intelligencer*) 'only like lopping the branches of a cornel tree, leaving the corrupting root to strike forth with greater strength than before'.[2] But that trade societies in some towns supported the Reform Bill is demonstrated by their participation in processions such as that at Edinburgh in protest against rejection of the Bill in 1831, and in Birmingham in triumph after the Lords finally gave way ([36] 177).

In general, however, it appears that the strongly organised trades did not play a direct part in the Reform Bill agitation, but that trade unionists in depressed trades were more inclined to do so. The same pattern is visible in the Chartist movement in the late 1830s and 1840s, though political involvement may have become rather wider. The Webbs considered that although 'the vast majority of manual-working wage-earners' supported the Chartist aims, the trade unions did not become 'part and parcel of the Movement'. A few trades, such as the shoemakers, became thoroughly permeated with Chartism, and the strikes of 1842 in Lancashire and the Midlands were briefly 'captured' by the Chartists, but there is little evidence of trade unions them-

[2] Briggs, loc. cit., pp. 312–13.

selves, as distinct from individual members, committing themselves or their funds to Chartism. The records of such societies as the bookbinders, compositors, ironfounders, cotton spinners, steam-engine makers and stonemasons contain no traces of Chartism; its violent, revolutionary aspects repelled such skilled 'aristocratic' artisans ([36] 174–7).

Hovell similarly concluded 'that the trade societies as a whole stood outside the Chartist movement, though many trade unionists were no doubt Chartists too' ([92] 169). The more recent *Chartist Studies*, edited by Briggs, have tended to confirm this view, providing only scattered evidence of trade-union involvement. During the past few years, however, left-wing writers have made persistent efforts to demonstrate the solidarity of the 'proletariat' and the 'revolutionary potential' of Chartism. The keenest debate has been on Chartism in London: on the one hand, Rowe has produced evidence to demonstrate the failure of London Chartism, especially the lack of support from the metropolitan trade societies [104], while Prothero, on the other hand, has marshalled equally impressive evidence to the contrary [102, 103]. There is now, however, some measure of agreement between these and other protagonists, that two broad distinctions must be made: firstly, chronological, in that up to 1840 Chartism was, on the whole, a failure in London, but that after that date there was a dramatic change, with much more widespread support; and secondly, social, in that whilst the 'upper' metropolitan trades, such as printers, bookbinders, engineers, coachmakers, goldsmiths, watchmakers, etc., favourably situated economically and socially superior, did not generally support Chartism at any time, the 'lower' trades, such as tailors, shoemakers, carpenters, and many others, relatively depressed economically and socially, became staunch adherents of Chartism and formed numerous Chartist associations in the 1840s. Moreover, these lower trades, because of their weakness, were also much more inclined to common trades' action, as in the National Association of United Trades in 1845 and later years; the stronger societies would only take combined action when faced with threatened legislation against all trade unions, as in 1825, 1838 and 1844.

To the present writer it appears that, while Prothero has certainly made a most valuable reinterpretation of metropolitan Chartism – and an equally valuable contribution to general trade-union studies, with his emphasis on the previous neglect of the weaker, declining trade societies, by comparison with the stronger, more successful ones – he has tended to exaggerate his case. He tends to inflate the numbers and importance of the 'lower', small-scale, handicraft trades, to whom, he suggests rather dubiously, primacy in the trade-union movement belonged in the first half of the nineteenth century, and among whom there was a marked tendency towards combined action and political agitation. By contrast, he underestimates the growth of large-scale industry in London and the numbers and importance of the 'upper' trades, both old and new, who were inclined to class collaboration, as Rowe has pointed out. At the same time, he minimises the sectional characteristics of the lower trades, and exaggerates the alleged predominance of the upper, so-called 'New Model' types after 1850. He tends, like Hobsbawm, to see a 'watershed' in about 1850, and to lay stress on the existence before that date of numerous depressed and increasingly class-conscious workers, followed after 1850 by the dominance of bourgeois-minded, sectionally selfish 'New Model' unions. For such a 'discontinuity' there is very little evidence (see above, pp. 15–21, and below, pp. 50–5).

Other contributors to this debate, notably Goodway (see the *Labour History Society Bulletin*, no. 20, spring 1970), have gone to much greater exaggerations in stressing the 'revolutionary potential' of the depressed 'proletariat' in the trade societies and Chartist organisations of this period. They are clearly disappointed and baffled, as Marx and Engels were, that a revolution did not actually occur in England at this time. They ignore all evidence of social improvement and fail to appreciate the broad realism of the trade societies.

Outside London, there has been a great deal of similar local research in recent years, which has confirmed the greater tendency on the part of depressed groups, such as handloom weavers, to participate in political activity. In Manchester, for example, Read has demonstrated that this was so, whilst also pointing out the more general trade-union support for Chartism in periods of intense trade depression, as in 1838 and 1842 [86] chap. 3). But his researches and those of A. G. Rose[3] and Turner ([71] 103–5) have shown that the Webbs were right in referring to the 'Plug Plot' strikes of 1842 as primarily trade unionist, fighting against wage reductions, and not political, although the Chartists attempted to 'capture' the strikes. Jenkin's attempt to give this abortive general strike a political, class-revolutionary significance is interesting but unconvincing [93]; it was basically economic and social, and the temporary enthusiasm of trade societies for the Charter was soon dissipated.

Mather's overall impression is that Chartism attracted most support in depressed handicraft trades, and comparatively little from the 'labour aristocracy', old or new, organised in strong unions [95]. Histories of trade unions in cotton-spinning, engineering, ironfounding, printing and pottery have also confirmed this impression, though there has been dispute as to the extent of Chartist influence in the Miners' Association (see the trade-union histories listed in the Bibliography). Pelling's general survey also indicates that the direct links between trade unions and Chartism were 'rather tenuous' except in severe slumps; as Chartism became more violent, 'it increasingly separated itself from . . . the trade unions as such' ([33] 34–5).

[3] A. G. Rose, 'The Plug Riots of 1842 in Lancashire and Cheshire', *Lancashire and Cheshire Antiquarian Society Transactions,* LXVII (1957).

6 *The 'Old Model' Strengthened*

ALTHOUGH the Webbs exaggerated the débâcle produced by the collapse of the 'Grand National', they recognised that 'the Trade Union Movement was not absolutely left for dead when Owen quitted the field' ([36] 168–79). In the trade boom of 1835–6, in fact, there was a good deal of union activity, including strikes by cotton spinners, potters, builders and engineers. This was followed, however, by severe depression, lasting until 1842–3, with heavy unemployment, wage reductions and loss of membership, which seriously weakened all trade societies. Nevertheless, the vigorous joint defence organised in support of the Glasgow cotton spinners and before the Select Commission on Combinations in 1837–8, and the widespread strikes in 1842, demonstrated that the movement was still by no means defunct.

Improving trade after 1842 led to the founding or revival of national unions among coal miners, cotton spinners, printers, potters, glassmakers, tailors, shoemakers and curriers in the mid-1840s, and the establishment of the National Association of United Trades in 1845 ([36] chap. 4). The histories of some of these unions, previously referred to, have confirmed the strength and continuity of this recovery, with its emphasis on sectional organisation and concentration on trade affairs. Prothero has tried to portray the National Association as 'the most notable new trade organisation in the forties', with its revival of 'general union' and its combination of industrial, social and political policies [103]; but whilst he has shown the considerable support which it received from the depressed or declining sections of the London trades, the facts cannot be disputed that it did not become widespread, that bigger, stronger unions would not give it their support, and that it gradually fizzled out. It was much less class-consciously aggressive than the earlier 'Grand National', but it too proved a failure.

The Webbs strongly emphasised the 'reaction against the

policy of reckless aggression which marked the Owenite inflation' ([36] 198). Having themselves previously inflated the 'revolutionary' aspects of the movements in 1833–4, they now stressed the 'new spirit' of the mid-1840s, and created a 'New Model' of trade unionism dating from the formation of the Amalgamated Society of Engineers in 1851. But the present writer has demonstrated that there is little if any justification for the term 'New Model', and that 'what occurred . . . in the fifties and sixties was not the creation of a "New Model", but a strengthening of the old' [31]. There was no radical change in organisation, not even in the engineers' society, which was modelled on that of the Journeymen Steam Engine and Machine Makers' Society, the 'Old Mechanics' [60]. The movement towards amalgamation or federation of local societies into wider district or national unions, with attempts at greater central control, had, as we have seen, begun much earlier in several trades, and it had become widespread in the late 1820s and early 1830s, followed by a similar movement in the mid-1840s. The A.S.E. was merely an outstandingly successful example of this trend. In other ways too, the so-called 'New Model' unions merely maintained the traditional characteristics of the old skilled craft unions: restriction of membership to apprenticed craftsmen, payment of high subscriptions and provision of friendly benefits were long-established features. Nor was there any change of objectives: craft societies had always pursued sectionalist trade policies regarding wages, hours, apprenticeship and the 'closed shop'. Concern with these practical trade affairs gives 'a basic continuity to trade unionism between the 1820s and the 1870s' ([31] 8).

A 'labour aristocracy' was not, as Hobsbawm and R. Harrison have argued, a new feature of trade unionism in the third quarter of the nineteenth century ([12] chap. 15; [113] chap. 1). The extent to which there was a loss of 'class consciousness', a narrowing of trade-union horizons, a retreat from wider political and social aims, has been grossly exaggerated. Trade societies had almost *always* been composed of 'labour aristocrats' – either of the old elite of skilled handicraftsmen or of the new elite of engineers, cotton spinners, etc. – and they had always been strongly sectional; these fundamental characteristics had always been far stronger than any emergent class consciousness, while Owenism and Chartism had never made any wide or deep impression upon them, especially on the stronger unions, except perhaps in brief periods of serious trade depression.

The Webbs' false contrast of the earlier class-revolutionary, recklessly aggressive unions with the pacific, bourgeois-minded 'New Model' type, which almost abandoned the strike weapon, has become another part of popular mythology. Moreover, it has recently received strong left-wing support from Hobsbawm and Harrison [12, 113]. This view of the so-called 'New Model' has become associated with the notion of class treachery, with alleged class collaboration between the 'labour aristocracy' and the capitalist bourgeoisie in this 'golden age' of British economic predominance and imperialism : whilst the capitalist rich got richer, the labour aristocracy also feathered their nest, at the expense of the labouring masses below them, from whom they were increasingly divided by widening wage differentials; thus they shared in the process of 'exploitation'.

With Hobsbawm's views regarding the 'labour aristocracy' we have already dealt (see above, pp. 20–1). Harrison has put forward similar arguments. Like Hobsbawm, he sees the predominance of the 'labour aristocracy' in the 'New Model' unions as a novel and reactionary development. He has opposed the present writer's views – though attributing them confusedly to Hugh Clegg ([113] 13) – and maintains that during the second quarter of the century 'the most conspicuous feature' of the labour movement had been 'the breaking down of traditional distinctions among the labouring poor', while during the third quarter 'attention shifted to the building-up, consolidation and sharpening of distinctions within the working class'; the labour movement, in fact, then underwent 'a massive transformation unequalled by any that have occurred before or since'.

For these remarkable statements, however, there is hardly a shred of evidence. On the contrary, as we have seen, there is a vast amount to demonstrate that there was no such tremendous 'discontinuity' or 'watershed' (to use Harrison's terms), that from its early origins trade unionism had been 'aristocratic' and sectional, confined to skilled artisans, that wages differentials and differences in outlook between them and the 'labouring poor' had always been considerable, and that the tendencies towards a 'mass' or class movement in early socialism and Chartism had not seriously altered these deeply-rooted trade-union characteristics. Harrison obviously considers Doherty's National Association and Owen's 'Grand National' to be the really important features of trade-union development in the earlier period; the craft societies were at that time, he considers, 'laggards in relation to the Trade Union movement as a whole', because they had 'stood aside from [these] attempts at general union'. (For Hobsbawm's similar views, see [12] 276.) But in fact the earlier 'labour aristocracy' were not just a minority standing apart from 'the Trade Union movement as a whole': their skilled trade societies comprised the great majority of trade-union membership, and it was largely because of their sectionalism and lack of support that the attempts at 'general union' so quickly collapsed. It was not only the later so-called 'New Model' unions which 'preferred a pedestrian success to an heroic failure'; so did most of the earlier trade societies.

Neither before nor after 1851, however, can it be said that these societies adopted a pacific, class-collaborationist policy in trade affairs. They had always, of course, tried to avoid strikes if possible, to prevent loss of work and wages and to safeguard their funds, and collective bargaining had long been developing. Strikes had always been regarded as a necessary evil, a weapon to be used only in the last resort. 'United to protect, but not combined to injure', or some similar phrase, had been a common motto of many earlier unions. This had not, however, prevented the occurrence of numerous strikes, nor does their number appear to have diminished very much, if at all, in the third quarter of the century. It is true that with the changing economic climate and with the growing strength of trade unions, many employers were readier to recognise and negotiate with them, while the movement towards conciliation and arbitration became stronger during these years, though its roots go back into the earlier period [119–24].

The central executives, gradually increasing their powers, certainly exercised tighter control and tried whenever possible to negotiate settlements, which contributed substantially to improving wages and preserving industrial peace; it is doubtful whether greater militancy, and greater industrial disruption, would have produced much greater gains. But the unions never abandoned the strike weapon, and no one who has looked at trade-union records or read the *Beehive* can be in any doubt as to the constant occurrence of industrial disputes during this period. The engineers inaugurated their amalgamation with a great industrial battle, and the builders' strike at the end of that decade is an even more famous conflict. These were only the most notable amongst a host of smaller ones.

Many years ago now, in a most perceptive piece of historical revision, G. D. H. Cole demonstrated not only that the so-called 'New Model' unions were less novel organisationally than the Webbs had made out, and that they were not so pacifist or capitalist-minded either, but also that the so-called 'New Model' unions – the amalgamated, centralised, craft societies – by no means dominated the whole trade-union movement. As in the past, there remained wide differences in union structures and policies. The so-called 'New Model' spread from the engineers to the ironfounders, the building trades (such as the carpenters and bricklayers) and some others; but in mining, cotton, metals manufactures, cabinet-making, tailoring, boot- and shoemaking and many other trades, little or no attempt was made to follow the 'New Model'. In many trades, both in London and the provinces, innumerable small local societies still existed, while in others, such as mining, district unions remained strong, and in cotton also a loose federal structure was adopted and the 'basic unit remained the autonomous local society' ([71] 109). Among the weavers, moreover, as Turner has shown ([71] chaps. 3–4), there was already a strong development, from mid-century onwards, of a 'mass' unionism usually associated with the 'New Unionism' of the 1880s and 1890s. Centralised activity in the miners' and cotton unions was mostly confined to efforts at obtaining mines and factory legislation, i.e. it was political, not industrial. Where industrial and financial centralisation was adopted, moreover, as in Halliday's Amalgamated Association of Miners, it was combined with an aggressively militant policy, quite unlike that usually regarded as characteristic of amalgamated 'New Model' societies.

Cole also discerned that the 'New Model' unions did not exercise such firm or widespread control over the whole trade-union movement as the Webbs asserted. The famous 'Junta' did not completely dominate even the London Trades Council, but were seriously challenged by the smaller, more militant metropolitan societies, led by George Potter, and, as we shall see, it was Potter, together with provincial trade-union leaders, who eventually created the T.U.C., in opposition to the 'Junta' (see below, pp. 61–2). The Webbs, in fact, viewing developments from London, greatly underestimated the importance, and the differing structures and policies, of provincial unions.

Furthermore, Cole also seriously questioned the view 'that with the decline of Chartism in the later 1840s the British Labour movement relapsed suddenly into an acquiescence in capitalist conditions of employment, and even into a belief in the inexorable laws of capitalist Political Economy'. That they were not socialist or revolutionary, he agreed – nor were most of the Chartists, and certainly not the earlier trade societies – but that did not mean that they accepted 'the philosophy of capitalism'. Cole's perception has again been confirmed by subsequent research, notably by Clements, who has demolished the Webbs' view that trade unionists in this period passively adopted middle-class economic philosophy [20]. Whatever lip-service they may have had paid to it, when it suited their purposes, they certainly did not, in fact, accept the wage-fund theory, or freedom of contract, or the immutability of the 'laws' of supply and demand, nor did they regard strikes as useless and harmful. Unions continued to pursue their traditional trade policies, endeavouring to peg up wages, to reduce hours of work, to enforce apprenticeship restrictions and to apply the 'closed shop' wherever they could, despite the tenets of economic theory, and they did not shrink from strikes to achieve these ends. It is true that they recognised the forces of supply and demand as affecting employment and wage-rates – hence their efforts to control the supply of labour, by their traditional apprentice restrictions and their new emigration schemes [125–7] – but these and their other policies were, of course, opposed to *laissez-faire* and a free labour market.

Harrison admits the force of all this historical evidence and reinterpretation, but he is nevertheless determined to maintain the Webbs' myth of the great mid-century discontinuity, centred on the 'labour aristocracy' and the 'New Model': 'however much the generally-accepted contrast needs to be refined, it remains a contrast which must be insisted upon' ([113] 19). Doubtless this is another of the great labour legends that will long be kept alive, but some left-wing writers have recognised its complete falsity. Thompson, as we have seen, has dismissed the myth of the new 'labour aristocracy' (see above, p. 16), while Allen agrees with the present writer that 'New Model Unionism ranks as a piece of historical fiction' ([19] 5).

There is also plentiful evidence of ideological and political continuities after 1851. As Thompson has pointed out, the Painite, non-socialist tradition remained generally predominant in British working-class Radicalism until the 1880s ([16] 104–5). He has also referred to the other equally persistent tradition of collaboration with middle-class Radicals in efforts to secure political reform (see above, pp. 16–17). This too continued in the third quarter of the century, as Frances Gillespie demonstrated many years ago [112]. She also pointed out, and Saville has since emphasised [116–18], that Chartism did not die in 1848 and that its political ideas continued to exert some influence. Harrison similarly recognises that there was some political continuity ([113] 19). On the one hand, he acknowledges that there were strong elements in Chartism, as exemplified in Lovett, closely akin to the later socio-political attitudes of 'New Model' unionists: just as moderate Chartists had been prepared to collaborate with the middle-class Radicals to secure Parliamentary and other reforms, so too were trade-union leaders in the 1850s and 1860s. On the other hand, Harrison points out that labour politics in this period were not so devoid of class consciousness, so docilely class-collaborationist, 'as has sometimes been supposed', and that the class-struggle aspects of Chartism still found some expression during these years. One way or the other, it would seem that there was not such a great 'discontinuity' at mid-century after all!

But one must beware of attaching too much importance to the political role of trade unions in this as in the earlier period. They were certainly very active on issues particularly affecting their own interests, such as the Labour Laws (see below, pp. 59–63), but more generally they maintained a non-political attitude, restricting themselves almost entirely to trade affairs. Certainly there is very little trace of social-revolutionary ideas. A few unions, including the engineers, were interested in Christian Socialism and the old idea of co-operative workshops in the early 1850s, but this interest soon fizzled out.

It was in the trades councils, rather than in individual trade unions, that trade unionists found political expression. These, to use the Webbs' phrase, were 'the political organs of the Labour world'. This was not, however, their primary function: they were mostly created to provide mutual support for local societies involved in strikes. Many of them had appeared sporadically in earlier years, as 'committees of trades delegates', to deal with some particular crisis, but disintegrating afterwards. It was on the London Trades Council (dating its continuous existence from 1860), and on the 'Junta' within it, that the Webbs concentrated their attention. On the provincial trades councils, growing in number from the late 1850s onwards, they merely provided a long footnote. Since then, however, much more attention has been given to them (see the relevant section in the Bibliography). Richards' pioneering general history has been followed, at a considerable distance, by histories of trades councils in a number of towns, including Aberdeen, Birmingham, Edinburgh, Glasgow, Liverpool, London, Sheffield and Wolverhampton. The main features emerging from these studies are that the primary function of these early trades councils was industrial; that the pattern of labour relations was closely related to the local industrial structure; and that in these bodies we also see what Saville calls 'the intermeshing of skilled trade unionism with the Radical tradition', and the emergence of a moderate 'Lib-Lab' political philosophy. Wider political issues, however, do not appear to have impinged much upon them, except in London, where agitation was organised not only on domestic questions, especially political reform, but also on international ones such as the American Civil War, the Polish question and Italian independence.

To explore all these interests, however, would take us away from the main history of trade unionism into that of the Labour political movement. It is by no means clear how far trade-union Radicals such as Odger, Applegarth, Cremer, Howell, etc., involved their respective unions in these more purely political activities: it appears that it was primarily as members of the Trades Council or of the Reform League that they played their political roles, though obviously the fact that they were trade-union leaders was the basis of their influence; they could hardly have engaged so vigorously in political activities without the support (even if only passive) of their unions, and they clearly recognised that working men could not obtain their just rights without political as well as industrial action. But they frequently expressed concern not to involve trade unions in political action outside their proper sphere, except on such issues as the Labour Laws and the franchise which directly and powerfully affected their interests. The Reform League had great difficulty, as Leventhal has shown ([115] 64–5), in overcoming 'the indifference of organised trade unionism'; it was mainly trade depression and the legal threats to trade unions in the years 1866–7 that finally impelled them into political action. And even then trade-union leaders remained essentially non-revolutionary, co-operating with middle-class Radicals, pacific and constitutional in their proceedings.

The influence of Karl Marx on British trade unions during these years appears to have been very limited [109–11]. Although the First International Working Men's Association was founded in London in 1864, with George Odger, secretary of the Trades Council, as its president, and William Cremer as its secretary, the main motive of the relatively small number of British trade unions which affiliated was the very limited one of preventing strike-breaking through the introduction of European labour, although there was certainly a wider and increasing interest in international democratic movements at the time. The membership of affiliated British trade unions never reached more than about 50,000, possibly less, out of a total trade-union membership at the time of perhaps 800,000. The unions which joined, such as the bricklayers, tailors, shoemakers, cabinet-makers, etc., were mostly in declining or vulnerable handicraft trades, mainly in London – much the same as had earlier sought salvation in Owenism and Chartism. Nor were these very assiduous in attendance or payment of subcriptions. Interest soon dwindled and affiliations ceased. Only one major union, the Carpenters and Joiners, could be persuaded to join. The decision to move the seat of its council to New York in 1872 was followed by the rapid collapse of the International in this country. Ideologically, it had made very little impact on British trade unionism: the 'proletarian revolution', which Marx believed to be imminent, showed no sign whatever of actually starting among the cautious, traditional, non-philosophical trade unionists of this era.

In the inaugural address of the First International, Marx argued that 'the misery of the working masses has not diminished from 1848 to 1864', but in fact the general standard of living had improved appreciably during that period. Harrison recognises that there was general improvement, though he argues that the 'labour aristocracy' got more than their fair share, while the working-class proportion of national income tended to decline, so that they were *relatively* worse off ([113] 22–3). But there were certainly no grounds for the Marxist theory of increasing 'immiseration'. Capitalist enterprise – technological, managerial and commercial – was, in fact, leading not to increased misery, but to large increases in national production and wealth. This wealth, it is true, was very unequally distributed, but 'Victorian prosperity' was gradually percolating downwards, so that the economic and social climate hardly favoured revolution. Instead, trade unionists saw real gains to be won in movements for increased wages and reduced working hours, and in alliance with middle-class Radicals for political and social reforms.

7 *The Fight for Legal Status*

THE Webbs' account of the struggle for legal status and free collective bargaining, in the late 1860s and early 1870s, has been substantially modified. The present writer has demonstrated [32], and Roberts [34] and Coltham [23] have confirmed, that they greatly exaggerated the dominant role of the so-called 'New Model' unions and of the 'Junta'. As we have seen, the alleged 'New Model' was by no means the universal pattern of trade-union development in the third quarter of the century: in London, there were many smaller, more militant societies, often opposed to the 'Junta', and in the provinces, where the 'Junta' had comparatively little influence, there were different organisations, with different policies, among miners, textile workers, etc. It was among these unions that the Trades Union Congress was to originate.

Since the Act of 1825 trade unions had ceased to be unlawful, but their actions, or the actions of their members, could easily be interpreted in the law courts as criminally 'molesting', 'intimidating', etc. Many prosecutions, in fact, continued to occur under the common law of conspiracy, as well as under the law of master and servant, as Daphne Simon has demonstrated ([15] chap. 6). Moreover, trade unions had not yet acquired secure legal status; registration under the Friendly Societies Act of 1855 was to prove deceptive.

Meanwhile, however, all seemed fairly well with the increasingly strong unions which were developing during these years of mid-Victorian prosperity. They had every reason to be satisfied with their sectional organisation, which was enabling them to achieve substantial improvements in wages, hours and working conditions. Nevertheless, they were not devoid of class consciousness or of feelings of solidarity when there were general threats to the whole movement, or when serious strikes occurred. Mutual assistance, as we have seen, was the main motive behind the trades councils. Efforts at 'general union', however, continued to prove unsuccessful. The National Association of United Trades, founded in 1845, lingered on into the 1860s, but soon ceased to be of any great significance. An attempted 'mass movement' and 'Labour Parliament' during the widespread strikes in Lancashire in 1853–4, in which Ernest Jones, the Chartist leader, played a leading part, also proved ephemeral. The builders' strike in London in 1859–60, however, over the nine-hour day and the 'document', again revived feelings of solidarity, resulting in the formation of the London Trades Council and receiving widespread support from the provinces. The Trades Council, moreover, soon broadened its activities (in accordance with the 1861 rules) 'to watch over the general interests of labour, political and social, both in and out of Parliament', and 'to use their influence in supporting any measure likely to benefit trades' unions'. Thus we find the Council campaigning in the early 1860s for amendment of the law of master and servant, for Conciliation and Arbitration Acts, for new Mines Regulation Acts, and other labour legislation, as well as in the broader field of Parliamentary reform and on international political questions (see above, p. 57). At the same time, of course, it continued to provide general assistance to societies involved in strikes.

Although unions continued to be predominantly sectional in trade affairs, and provincial trades councils remained primarily local strike-support organisations, there was an increasing tendency during the 1860s towards more general action, especially in the political field. This was mainly because the trade-union movement as a whole became increasingly aware of 'the legal restraints under which it operated' ([112] 227; [107]). It was the Glasgow Trades Council which initiated the campaign in the early 1860s which led to a national conference in London in May 1864 – attended by delegates from many individual unions as well as from trades councils – followed by a political campaign which led to a modified, though still unsatisfactory, Master and Servant Act in 1867. Another Act that same year, for the establishment of Courts of Conciliation and Arbitration, was also an outcome of this conference and subsequent trade-union pressure.

Meanwhile, within the London Trades Council, divisions developed between the 'Junta' and the large amalgamated societies, on the one hand, and the smaller, more old-fashioned and militant metropolitan societies, led by George Potter, on the other. Potter, controlling the *Beehive*, built up substantial support and established the rival London Working Men's Association, which gave enthusiastic support to strikes, both in London and the provinces. They also supported the efforts of the Wolverhampton and Sheffield trades councils in arranging another national trades' conference, in Sheffield, in July 1866, on the occasion of a lock-out in the Sheffield file trade, in order to establish 'a national organisation among the trades of the United Kingdom, for the purpose of effectually resisting all lock-outs'. This resulted in the formation of another national trades' federation – the 'United Kingdom Alliance of Organised Trades' – for mutual support in lock-outs, but Courts of Conciliation and Arbitration were also advocated, together with reform of the law of master and servant. This federation, however, proved no more successful than previous attempts: further conferences were held in 1867 and 1871, but membership fell rapidly because of internal dissensions, strike failures and inadequate funds, and the Alliance soon ceased to be of any real importance.

Meanwhile, the notorious 'outrages' occurred in Sheffield [6], where the Alliance had its headquarters, and also in Manchester, and the resultant public outcry led to the appointment of a Royal Commission of Inquiry into trade unions in February 1867. At the same time, the famous *Hornby* v. *Close* decision in the Court of Queen's Bench in January deprived trade unions of their imagined legal status under the Friendly Societies Act, and also raised again the question as to whether trade unions, acting 'in restraint of trade', were illegal.

In this emergency, the whole trade-union movement rose in its own defence, but the leadership was divided. The 'Junta' formed the 'Conference of Amalgamated Trades', but they were challenged by Potter and his supporters, who organised another national trades' conference in London in March 1867, with strong representation from the provinces. It is clear that the Webbs greatly underestimated the extent of opposition – both metropolitan and provincial – to the cliquish control of the 'Junta'. Their London-centred interests also caused them to deal very inadequately – merely in a long footnote – with the establishment of the Trades Union Congress, summoned by the Manchester and Salford Trades Council in a circular of 21 February 1868. This was not intended to be a trades' federation – the United Kingdom Alliance being still in existence – but was an entirely new departure, as an annual congress of trade unions and trades councils. Previously they had failed to obtain a fair hearing in such middle-class bodies as the Social Science Association; so Samuel Nicholson, treasurer of the Manchester typographical society and president of the local trades council, suggested that trade unions should hold an annual congress of their own, for discussion not only of subjects particularly affecting them, such as trade-union legislation, but also of wider political and social affairs, including factory legislation, education, etc., with the idea of mobilising trade-union opinion and bringing pressure on Parliament.

The main concern of this first Congress, held in Manchester early in June 1868, was, of course, the Royal Commission and the legal position of trade unions. But the Conference of Amalgamated Trades in London continued to operate, and the rift in the trade-union leadership was not finally closed until the third Congress, held in London in March 1871. The trade unions, then fully organised on a national basis, with control in the hands of the T.U.C. Parliamentary Committee, were able to organise a powerful political agitation and to achieve their legislative objectives: firstly, the Trade Union Act of 1871, which gave them a secure legal status as registered societies; secondly, abolition of the Criminal Law Amendment Act (1871) and the passing of the Conspiracy and Protection of Property Act of 1875, which finally ended special criminal legislation relating to trade unions and put them under the ordinary law of the land,

permitting peaceful picketing, etc.; and thirdly, the Employers and Workmen Act, also of 1875, which abolished the old law of master and servant and made employers and workmen equal parties to a civil contract. Thus trade unions had finally achieved full legal recognition and freedom to carry out peaceful trade-union practices in collective bargaining and strikes.

8 *New Horizons*

IN the records of individual unions, these national movements occupy only a very small part. Sectional concerns with trade affairs and friendly benefits fill most of the pages in their minute-books and annual reports. Their national executives were gradually acquiring more control over trade affairs, but bargaining on these matters continued to be at branch and workshop level; it was not until the late nineteenth and early twentieth centuries that national negotiations and agreements developed, leading to a much greater loss of local autonomy. But, of course, behind the branches and workshops were the financial resources, control and negotiating skill of the union executives and general secretaries. Although many societies were still on a local or district level, and sometimes very small, the trend was towards amalgamation and bigger unions.

These unions still remained sectional and exclusive, composed of skilled workers and still, in many trades, insistent on apprenticeship qualifications. Towards the end of this period, however, especially in the tremendous boom of the early 1870s, unions began to be formed among semi-skilled workers and labourers. This was not an entirely new phenomenon: there had long previously been examples of ephemeral unionism among riverside and dock workers, keelmen and seamen, gas stokers, railway workers and agricultural labourers, especially in periods of general labour ferment, social distress and political excitement, as in the early 1830s, when they helped to swell the 'mob', participated in riots, and even attempted union organisation; but the great mass of these lower-paid, largely illiterate and inarticulate workers had remained outside the ranks of formal and continuous trade unionism. Now, however, trade-union ideas were penetrating more deeply and spreading more widely. Indeed, in the early 1870s we can discern the growth of 'New Unionism' – the organising of these lower-paid workers into 'industrial' or 'general' unions – usually associated with the movements among dockers, gasworkers, match-girls, etc., in the late 1880s.

Hobsbawm was among the first to emphasise that this expansion of the early 1870s was 'an important – and neglected – forerunner of the "New Unionism" ' of the 1880s ([12] chaps. 10–11). Lovell has stressed it even more strongly: 'masses of labourers in many parts of the country and in many occupations flocked to join unions in the early 1870s. Railwaymen, seamen, carmen, agricultural labourers, gas workers as well as port workers were involved', with widespread strikes for increased wages ([75] 59–76). Among the London dockers, for example, in 1871–2 the 'Labour Protection League' was established, 'in almost every respect as significant an organisation as the Dockers' Union founded seventeen years later'. There was even an attempt at organising a great transport workers' federation, an 'Amalgamated Labour Union', really a loose federation of dockers, carmen, lightermen and railway workers. But this and other attempts at 'general union' proved abortive, and greater success was achieved by unions of a sectional or industrial type. Permanent unions were established, for example, among the stevedores and the watermen and lightermen, akin to the skilled craft unions. The Engine Drivers' and Firemen's Society, formed in 1866, was of a similiar type, though short-lived, while the Amalgamated Society of Railway Servants (1871) tended to cater for the higher grades of railway workers. The gas stokers also formed their own separate union; Patrick Kenney's General Labourers' Amalgamated Union was primarily for builders' labourers; and most famous of all was Joseph Arch's National Agricultural Labourers' Union. All of these were founded in 1872 ([33] 72–7).

Perhaps the most notable feature of these developments in the lower ranks of the working classes was the replacement of rioting by generally peaceful union organisation. Improving literacy and communications were widening social and political awareness. But most of these unions were heavily reliant on outside help, e.g. from the Land and Labour League and from the older organised trades. Moreover, as in the past, they were products of booming trade, and when the 'Great Depression' began in the later 1870s most of them either collapsed or were reduced to insignificance, so that the next great forward movement, in the late 1880s, had to begin again, almost from the bottom; only among the more skilled and better-paid of these workers does trade unionism appear to have struck permanent root. Nevertheless, 'New Unionism' was born.

Another development of great potential significance was the revival of working-class political organisation during the campaigns of the 1860s and early 1870s for Parliamentary reform and full legalisation of trade unions. These gave rise to increased class consciousness. The Reform League, founded in opposition to the middle-class Reform Union – though with important middle-class Radical support, both intellectual and financial – was followed, after the 1867 Reform Act, by the establishment in 1869 of the Labour Representation League, the chief aim of which was 'to secure the return to Parliament of qualified working men'; most of its executive were leading trade unionists in London. This, as the Webbs pointed out, was 'a most significant symptom of the new feeling in Labour politics' ([36] 287). It signified growing dissatisfaction with the upper- and middle-class structure of the Liberal and Conservative parties and of Parliament. Moreover, individual trade unions, such as the miners and ironworkers, also took up the idea and at the 1874 election there were thirteen 'Labour candidates', of whom two, Alexander Macdonald and Thomas Burt, the two leading officials of the National Union of Miners, became the first 'Labour members' of the House of Commons.

The Labour Representation League, however, tended to be associated with the Liberal Party. Hence the establishment of a left-wing rival organisation, the Land and Labour League, also founded in 1869, and notable for its links with the International, its proposals for land nationalisation and its efforts at organising unskilled workers. Harrison has tended to inflate its importance, describing it as advancing 'by leaps and bounds' in the early 1870s, its 'militant policies . . . everywhere in the ascendant'; but, as he observes, 'it soon ceased to make . . . real headway' and rapidly declined in the later 1870s. It was, in fact, an extremist minority movement. Nevertheless, it certainly did anticipate 'future lines of development' in the 1880s – the movement towards socialism and 'New Unionism' ([113] chap. 5).

After the Parliamentary triumphs of 1875, however, trade-union political activity dwindled. Interest was limited to such matters as factory legislation, employers' liability, etc., and there was a return to traditional 'Lib-Labism'. In the trade depression of the later 1870s, unions tended to withdraw defensively into their sectional shells. But the foundations of trade unionism were now firmly established, a solid base for future developments, both industrial and political.

Hobsbawm, despite his dislike of the sectional, 'aristocratic' features of the skilled unions, recognises their achievements ([12] 323). They had fought against capitalist employers for a greater share in profits and the reduction of working hours; they had established sound union organisation and finances; they had worked out skilful bargaining tactics; they had formed trades councils and the Trades Union Congress; they had secured the legal status of trade unions and other useful social reforms. But they were non-revolutionary: 'the British labour movement was formed and moulded at this time when the dominant tradition was that of reforming liberal-radicalism, whose stamp it still bears' ([12] 341). Marxists, of course, consider this a vice; others may regard it as a virtue.

Select Bibliography

For clarity of presentation, books and articles have been arranged in sections, covering different aspects, with brief comments at the beginning of each section.

ORIGINAL DOCUMENTS

Surviving trade-union records (minute-books, reports, etc.) are very scanty before the middle of the nineteenth century, with the notable exception of the printing industry (see [62]). But a great deal of information has been gleaned from other sources, such as the Home Office papers (from which Aspinall has made an invaluable selection), Parliamentary inquiries, trade-union and radical periodicals, pamphlets, etc. Many trade-union documents have been included in collections relating to general working-class history, of which the most notable is that of Cole and Filson. The crisis facing trade unions in the late 1860s has been documented by Pollard and by Frow and Katanka.

[1] A. Aspinall, *The Early English Trade Unions* (1949).
[2] G. D. H. Cole and A. W. Filson, *British Working-Class Movements: Select Documents, 1789–1875* (1951).
[3] E. Frow and M. Katanka, *1868: Year of the Unions* (1968).
[4] J. B. Jefferys, *Labour's Formative Years, 1849–1879* (1948).
[5] M. Morris, *From Cobbett to the Chartists, 1815–48* (1948).
[6] S. Pollard, *The Sheffield Outrages* (1971).

GENERAL LABOUR HISTORIES

Trade-union developments have often been included in general histories of working-class movements, covering wider political and social aspects. Works written a generation or two ago by such scholars as Beer and Cole are still among the best, but they have been supplemented and modified by recent contributions, of which the most outstanding (and most controversial) is that of Thompson. Many of Hobsbawm's discerning (and also controversial) articles have been brought together in his *Labouring Men*, while the essays edited by Briggs and Saville have illuminated various aspects of labour history.

[7] M. Beer, *A History of British Socialism*, 3rd ed. (2 vols, 1953).
[8] A. Briggs and J. Saville (eds), *Essays in Labour History*, vol. I (2nd ed., 1967).
[9] W. H. Chaloner, *The Skilled Artisan during the Industrial Revolution, 1750–1850* (Historical Association pamphlet, 1969).
[10] G. D. H. Cole, *A Short History of the British Working Class Movement* (1948).
[11] J. L. and B. Hammond, *The Skilled Labourer, 1760–1832* (1919).
[12] E. J. Hobsbawm, *Labouring Men* (1964).
[13] W. H. Marwick, *A Short History of Labour in Scotland* (1967).
[14] J. Saville, 'A Note on the Present Position of Working Class History', *Yorkshire Bulletin of Economic and Social Research*, IV 2 (Sep 1952).
[15] J. Saville (ed.), *Democracy and the Labour Movement* (1954).
[16] E. P. Thompson, *The Making of the English Working Class*, rev. ed. (1968).
[17] J. T. Ward (ed.), *Popular Movements c. 1830–1850* (1970).
[18] R. F. Wearmouth, *Methodism and the Working-Class Movements of England, 1800–1850* (1937).

WORKS ON THE GENERAL HISTORY OF TRADE UNIONISM

The Webbs' great *History* is, of course, outstanding, but has been modified in many respects. Pelling's is the best recent general survey, but Cole made some of the most perceptive revisions, followed by a number of modern scholars.

[19] V. L. Allen, 'A Methodological Criticism of the Webbs as Trade Union Historians', *Labour History Society Bulletin*, no. 4 (spring 1962).
[20] R. V. Clements, 'British Trade Unions and Popular Political Economy, 1850–1875', *Economic History Review*, 2nd ser., XIV 1 (Aug 1961).
[21] G. D. H. Cole, 'Some Notes on British Trade Unionism in the Third Quarter of the Nineteenth Century', *International Review for Social History*, II (1937), reprinted in E. M. Carus-Wilson (ed.), *Essays in Economic History*, vol. III (1962).
[22] G. D. H. Cole, *Attempts at General Union, 1818–1834* (1953).
[23] S. W. Coltham, 'George Potter, the Junta, and the

Beehive', *International Review of Social History*, IX (1964) and X (1965).
[24] I. Garbati, 'British Trade Unionism in the Mid-Victorian Era', *University of Toronto Quarterly*, XX (1950–1).
[25] M. D. George, 'The Combination Laws Reconsidered', *Economic History* (supplement to *Economic Journal*), no. 2 (May 1927).
[26] M. D. George, 'The Combination Laws', *Economic History Review*, VI (1936).
[27] R. Y. Hedges and A. Winterbottom, *The Legal History of Trade Unionism* (1930).
[28] E. J. Hobsbawm, 'Trade Union Historiography', *Labour History Society Bulletin*, no. 8 (spring 1964).
[29] H. W. McCready, 'British Labour and the Royal Commission on Trade Unions, 1867–9', *University of Toronto Quarterly*, XXIV (1955).
[30] H. W. McCready, 'British Labour's Lobby, 1867–75', *Canadian Journal of Economic and Political Science*, XXII (1956).
[31] A. E. Musson, 'The Webbs and their Phasing of Trade-Union Development between the 1830s and the 1860s', *Labour History Society Bulletin*, no. 4 (spring 1962).
[32] A. E. Musson, *The Congress of 1868: The Origins and Establishment of the Trades Union Congress* (1955; rev. ed., 1968).
[33] H. M. Pelling, *A History of British Trade Unionism* (1963).
[34] B. C. Roberts, *The Trades Union Congress, 1868–1921* (1958).
[35] M. I. Thomis, *The Luddites* (1970).
[36] S. and B. Webb, *The History of Trade Unionism*, rev. ed. (1920).
[37] S. and B. Webb, *Industrial Democracy* (1920).

HISTORIES OF TRADE UNIONS IN PARTICULAR INDUSTRIES

General histories of trade unionism mostly deal only with broad trends and outstanding episodes. To appreciate the fundamental and continuous trade-union characteristics, the practical problems arising from their industrial environment, the variations in structure and policy, the detailed organisation, methods of collective bargaining and strikes, as well as administration of friendly benefits – in fact, to get the real atmosphere and 'feel' of trade unionism – it is necessary to read a fairly wide selection of trade-union histories, soundly based on trade-union records.

Agriculture

[38] J. P. D. Dunbabin, 'The "Revolt of the Field": The Agricultural Labourers' Movement in the 1870s', *Past and Present*, no. 26 (1963).

[39] R. Groves, *'Sharpen the Sickle!': The History of the Farm Workers' Union* (1949).

[40] E. J. Hobsbawm and G. Rudé, *Captain Swing* (1969).

[41] A. J. Peacock, 'The Revolt of the Field in East Anglia', in L. M. Munby (ed.), *The Luddites and Other Essays* (1971).

[42] R. C. Russell, *The 'Revolt of the Field' in Lincolnshire* (1956).

[43] Trades Union Congress, *The Book of the Martyrs of Tolpuddle, 1834–1934* (1934).

Brushmaking

[44] W. Kiddier, *The Old Trade Unions* (1930).

Building, woodworking, etc.

[45] T. J. Connelly, *The Woodworkers, 1860–1960* (Amalgamated Society of Woodworkers, 1960).

[46] J. O. French, *Plumbers in Unity: History of the Plumbing Trades Union, 1865–1965* (1965).

[47] S. Higenbottam, *Our Society's History* (Amalgamated Society of Woodworkers, 1939).

[48] W. S. Hilton, *Foes to Tyranny: A History of the Amalgamated Union of Building Trade Workers* (1963).

[49] R. Postgate, *The Builders' History* (1923).

Coal mining

[50] R. Challinor and B. Ripley, *The Miners' Association: A Trade Union in the Age of the Chartists* (1968).

[51] N. Edwards, *History of the South Wales Miners* (1926).

[52] E. W. Evans, *The Miners of South Wales* (1961).

[53] F. Machin, *The Yorkshire Miners: A History*, vol. I (1958).

[54] A. J. Taylor, 'The Miners' Association of Great Britain and Ireland, 1842–48', *Economica*, n.s., XXII (1955).

[55] S. Webb, *The Story of the Durham Miners, 1662–1921* (1921).

[56] E. Welbourne, *The Miners' Unions of Northumberland and Durham* (1923).

[57] J. E. Williams, *The Derbyshire Miners* (1962).

[58] A. J. Youngson-Brown, 'Trade Union Policy in the Scots Coalfields, 1855–1885', *Economic History Review*, 2nd ser., VI 1 (Aug 1953).

Iron and engineering
[59] H. J. Fyrth and H. Collins, *The Foundry Workers* (1959).
[60] J. B. Jefferys, *The Story of the Engineers, 1800–1945* (1946).

Pottery
[61] W. H. Warburton, *History of Trade Union Organisation in the North Staffordshire Potteries* (1931).

Printing and bookbinding
[62] E. Howe, *The London Compositor: Documents* (1947).
[63] E. Howe and H. E. Waite, *The London Society of Compositors: A Centenary History* (1948).
[64] E. Howe and J. Child, *The London Society of Bookbinders, 1780–1951* (1952).
[65] A. E. Musson, *The Typographical Association: Origins and History up to 1949* (1954).

Textiles and clothing
[66] D. Bythell, *The Handloom Weavers* (1969).
[67] N. H. Cuthbert, *The Lace Makers' Society: A Study of Trade Unionism in the British Lace Industry, 1760–1960* (1960).
[68] F. W. Galton, *Select Documents Illustrating the History of Trade Unionism*, vol. I: *The Tailoring Trade* (1896).
[69] N. J. Smelser, *Social Change in the Industrial Revolution: An Application of Theory to the British Cotton Industry* (1959).
[70] M. Stewart and L. Hunter, *The Needle is Threaded* (1964).
[71] H. A. Turner, *Trade Union Growth, Structure and Policy: A Comparative Study of the Cotton Unions* (1962).

Transport and docks
[72] G. W. Alcock, *Fifty Years of Railway Trade Unionism* (1922).
[73] P. S. Bagwell, *The Railwaymen: The History of the National Union of Railwaymen* (1963).
[74] P. W. Kingsford, *Victorian Railwaymen: The Emergence and Growth of Railway Labour, 1830–1870* (1970).
[75] J. Lovell, *Stevedores and Dockers* (1969).

HISTORIES OF TRADE UNIONISM AND TRADES COUNCILS IN PARTICULAR TOWNS

Modern trade unionism is national, based on particular industries, or particular industrial sections, or (in the case of general unions) upon groups of related industrial occupations. But for much of the nineteenth century trade unionism was local; even after national unions were formed, local branches still retained a good deal of autonomy. At the local level too, long before the Trades Union Congress was founded, trade societies were accustomed to collaborate. But only recently have historians begun to study trade unionism in particular towns. Pollard's history of labour in Sheffield is the most outstanding example, but a number of histories of trades councils have now appeared.

[76] G. Barnsby, *The Origins of Wolverhampton Trades Council* (1965).
[77] J. Corbett, *The Birmingham Trades Council, 1866–1966* (1966).
[78] A. Fox, 'Industrial Relations in 19th century Birmingham', *Oxford Economic Papers*, n.s., VII (1955).
[79] W. Hamling, *A Short History of the Liverpool Trades' Council, 1848–1948* (1948).
[80] I. MacDougall, *The Minutes of Edinburgh Trades Council, 1859–1873* (1968).
[81] S. Pollard, *A History of Labour in Sheffield* (1959).
[82] S. Pollard *et al.*, *Sheffield Trades and Labour Council, 1858–1958* (1958).
[83] C. Richards, *A History of Trades Councils* (1920).
[84] J. Saville, 'Trades Councils and the Labour Movement to 1900', *Labour History Society Bulletin*, no. 14 (spring 1967).
[85] G. Tate, *The London Trades Council, 1860–1950* (1950).

TRADE-UNION RELATIONS WITH THE OWENITE-SOCIALIST, RADICAL AND CHARTIST MOVEMENTS

These aspects of working-class history have attracted an immense amount of attention, but their relationship to trade unionism has not, until recently, been very thoroughly investigated. The Webbs' exaggeration, for example, of the impact of Owenite socialism on trade unionism has been frequently but uncritically repeated. Similarly, there has not, until recent years, been any serious study of the connections between the Radical–Chartist movements and trade unions. We have only included here, therefore, such works as throw some light on these interrelationships. Readers should also consult the general and specialised histories listed in previous sections.

[86] A. Briggs (ed.), *Chartist Studies* (1959).
[87] G. D. H. Cole, *Robert Owen* (1925).
[88] M. I. Cole, *Robert Owen of New Lanark* (1953).

[89] W. H. Fraser, 'Robert Owen and the Workers', in J. Butt (ed.), *Robert Owen* (1971).
[90] B. Harrison and P. Hollis, 'Chartism, Liberalism and the Life of Robert Lowery', *English Historical Review*, LXXXII (1967).
[91] J. F. C. Harrison, *Robert Owen and the Owenites in Britain and America* (1969).
[92] M. Hovell, *The Chartist Movement* (1918; 3rd ed., 1966).
[93] A. Jenkin, 'Chartism and the Trade Unions', in L. M. Munby (ed.), *The Luddites and Other Essays* (1971).
[94] H. Maehl, 'Chartist Disturbances in Northeastern England, 1839', *International Review of Social History*, VIII (1963).
[95] F. C. Mather, *Chartism* (Historical Association pamphlet, 1965).
[96] A. E. Musson, 'The Ideology of Early Co-operation in Lancashire and Cheshire', *Lancashire and Cheshire Antiquarian Society Transactions*, LXVIII (1958).
[97] R. S. Neale, 'Class and Class-Consciousness in Early Nineteenth-Century England: Three Classes or Five?', *Victorian Studies*, XII (1968).
[98] W. H. Oliver, 'Robert Owen and the English Working-Class Movements', *History Today*, VIII (1958).
[99] W. H. Oliver, 'The Consolidated Trades' Union of 1834', *Economic History Review*, 2nd ser., XVII 1 (Aug 1964).
[100] F. Podmore, *Robert Owen* (2 vols, 1906).
[101] S. Pollard and J. Salt (eds), *Robert Owen: Prophet of the Poor* (1971).
[102] I. Prothero, 'Chartism in London', *Past and Present*, no. 44 (Aug 1969).
[103] I. Prothero, 'London Chartism and the Trades', *Economic History Review*, 2nd ser., XXIV 2 (May 1971).
[104] D. J. Rowe, 'The Failure of London Chartism', *Historical Journal*, XI (1968).
[105] D. J. Rowe, 'Class and Political Radicalism in London, 1831–2', *Historical Journal*, XIII (1970).
[106] G. Rudé, 'English Rural and Urban Disturbances on the Eve of the First Reform Bill, 1830–1831', *Past and Present*, no. 37 (1967).

TRADE UNIONS, POLITICS AND SOCIETY, 1850–75

The most outstanding work in this field is still the pioneering study of Frances Gillespie, written nearly half a century ago, but

Royden Harrison has more recently made some important contributions, collected in *Before the Socialists*, while Collins and Abramsky have investigated the influence of Karl Marx and the First International on the British labour movement, and Leventhal has just produced an excellent biographical study of George Howell. Again, readers should also consult the general and special works listed in previous sections.

[107] C. F. Brand, 'The Conversion of the British Trade-Unions to Political Action', *American Historical Review*, xxx 2 (Jan 1925).

[108] A. Briggs, 'Robert Applegarth and the Trade Unions', in *Victorian People* (1954).

[109] H. J. Collins and C. Abramsky, *Karl Marx and the British Labour Movement: Years of the First International* (1965).

[110] H. J. Collins, 'The English Branches of the First International', in Briggs and Saville [8].

[111] H. J. Collins, 'The International and the British Labour Movement', *Labour History Society Bulletin*, no. 9 (autumn 1964).

[112] F. E. Gillespie, *Labor and Politics in England, 1850–1867* (1927; reprinted 1968).

[113] R. Harrison, *Before the Socialists: Studies in Labour and Politics, 1861–1881* (1965).

[114] A. W. Humphrey, *Robert Applegarth* (1913).

[115] F. M. Leventhal, *Respectable Radical: George Howell and Victorian Working Class Politics* (1971).

[116] J. Saville, *Ernest Jones: Chartist* (1952).

[117] J. Saville, 'The Background to the Revival of Socialism in England', *Labour History Society Bulletin*, no. 11 (autumn 1965).

[118] J. Saville, 'Some Aspects of Chartism in Decline', *Labour History Society Bulletin*, no. 20 (spring 1970).

INDUSTRIAL CONCILIATION AND ARBITRATION

From the Combination Act of 1800 onwards there has been legislation intended to encourage settlement of industrial disputes by conciliation and arbitration. Efforts to devise such machinery by trade unions and employers' associations became increasingly numerous in the second half of the nineteenth century.

[119] V. L. Allen, 'The Origins of Industrial Conciliation and

Arbitration', *International Review of Social History*, IX (1964).
[120] R. A. Church, 'Technological Change and the Hosiery Board of Conciliation and Arbitration, 1860–1884', *Yorkshire Bulletin of Economic and Social Research*, XV (1963).
[121] J. R. Hicks, 'The Early History of Industrial Conciliation in England', *Economica*, X (1930).
[122] A. J. Odber, 'The Origins of Industrial Peace: The Manufactured Iron Trade of the North of England', *Oxford Economic Papers*, n.s., III (1951).
[123] J. H. Porter, 'Wage Bargaining under Conciliation Agreements, 1860–1914', *Economic History Review*, n.s., XXIII 3 (Dec 1970).
[124] I. G. Sharp, *Industrial Conciliation and Arbitration in Great Britain* (1950).

TRADE UNIONS AND EMIGRATION

Trade-union emigration schemes were a marked feature of the third quarter of the nineteenth century. Erickson and Shepperson consider them to be a means of reducing labour supply, while Clements regards them rather as a form of relief for unemployed and striking members.

[125] R. V. Clements, 'Trade Unions and Emigration, 1840–80', *Population Studies*, IX (1955).
[126] C. Erickson, 'The Encouragement of Emigration by British Trade Unions, 1850–1900', *Population Studies*, III (1949–50).
[127] W. S. Shepperson, 'Industrial Emigration in Early Victorian Britain', *Journal of Economic History*, XIII (1953).

Index